THE POLITICAL CULTURES OF MASSACHUSETTS

THE POLITICAL CULTURES OF MASSACHUSETTS

EDGAR LITT

THE M.I.T. PRESS
MASSACHUSETTS INSTITUTE OF TECHNOLOGY
CAMBRIDGE, MASSACHUSETTS, AND LONDON, ENGLAND

Library of Congress Catalog Card Number 65-26663
Printed in the United States of America

To Vivienne and Martin Dean
who have enriched the Bay State and the
life of one of its political analysts

ACKNOWLEDGMENTS

There are three scholars who, over the years, have taught me most of what I know about the uses of political imagination and political knowledge. Whatever value this book may have is due, in large measure, to enriching dialogues with Ralph K. Huitt, Robert E. Lane, and Earl Latham. In addition, a number of people have given generously of their time and ideas. They have included the late Professor V. O. Key, Jr., Professors Kermit Morissey, Henry Pratt, Allan Schick, Bradbury Seasholes, and James Q. Wilson. I am especially grateful to Professor Robert C. Wood for his critical review of the complete manuscript. Mr. Lester Hyman, former Advisor to Governor Endicott Peabody, State Representative George M. O'Farrell (Democrat, Malden), State Representative Freyda P. Koplow (Republican, Brookline), and Congressman Thomas P. O'Neill (Democrat, Cambridge) have also been most helpful.

Professor Josephine Milburn and her students in Political Parties at Simmons College collaborated with me and a similar group at Boston College in the 1962 Boston Political Survey, an endeavor that contributed much to this study. I am most grateful for their assistance.

The editors have kindly permitted me to draw on two of my articles, "Political Futility and Political Cynicism," *The Journal of Politics,* (May 1963), and "Civic Education,

Community Norms, and Political Indoctrination," *American Sociological Review,* (February 1963). Grants from the Boston College Faculty Fund and the National Center For Education in Politics were also most helpful.

Mrs. Ellen S. Heller, Mr. Carroll Newquist, and Mr. Jack Bell prepared the manuscript with skill and care. It was my wife, Vivienne, who made it possible for me to write this book in the first place.

March, 1965

EDGAR LITT

CONTENTS

LIST OF TABLES

Table		Page

INTRODUCTION

MASSACHUSETTS: THE ENDURING IMAGE AND THE CHANGING REALITY

The time has passed when state politics could be studied in isolation from national economic and political forces: distinct ethnic, public, and regional features are no longer the major contributors to the quality of politics in the Bay State, and new intellectual premises are needed to assess the impact of recent cultural changes.

The meaning of legislative, gubernatorial, and party politics in Massachusetts today is found in the conflict between the old and the new cultures. The old culture was rooted in rural and industrial patterns. The new culture is a product of the national political economy and its emphasis on technological, social, and political management.

The governor, once the champion of the industrial workers and the ethnic minority groups, is now more closely allied with the growing suburbs and their political demands. The legislature, once the bastion of Republican opposition to the New Deal policies of Democratic governors, is now the stronghold of local rural and core-city interests dislocated by the new organizational society. The Republican Party, once the property of patrician State Street businessmen, is no longer a cohesive political instrument. The Democratic Party, once the major vehicle of the workingman, is now more responsive to new organizational techniques and middle-class political figures. Stalemates in public policy over taxation and education testify to the political potency of major groups within a decentralized government where it is easier to veto policy than to initiate it.

Massachusetts state government is highly decentralized because it serves a myriad of particular interests, especially those whose economic and cultural base has declined. Proposals for "reforms" in governmental and party structures are advanced by taxpayers' groups, the League of Women Voters, and academics assembled in suburban conclaves on state government. They are resisted by core-city and rural politicians, small businessmen, contractors, and local labor leaders — the enduring constituency of state government which most relies on it as a buffer against changes initiated by the major bureaucracies and institutions associated with the national political economy. The old feudal system of Massachusetts politics is crumbling along with the political hegemony of the cities and small towns that nurtured it. The Democratic state ticket was defeated in 1964, despite the Johnson-Kennedy landslide, primarily because the Massachusetts Democrats had failed to absorb the lesson of the preceding gubernatorial contests: a winning Democratic coalition can no longer be built on the working class and the ethnic minorities in the cities. A four-year gubernatorial term, and limitations on the power of the Executive Council to frustrate the governor, have been approved by the electorate, despite the opposition of the yeomen and the senior legislators from the cities functioning like a national conservative-Southern Democratic alliance. The newer alliances between the patrician and managerial cultures can be understood in the context of the contemporary political economy which is uprooting local customs and traditions.

This cultural orientation seeks to dispel some of the ambiguous images of the Massachusetts political legacy. On the one hand, there is the propriety of the Puritan tradition and, on the other, the claim that Massachusetts exceeds most of her sister states in political corruption. The Massachusetts electorate is thought to be deeply involved in the ethos of the town meeting, and yet to be especially alienated from the levers of political power.

Managerialism is a tendency observable in many areas of society — one thinks of the "managerial revolution," the literature on the organization man, and the growing political involvement of the professional class. However, in Massachusetts, managerialism and the professional classes who sponsor it are resisted by the legacy of class, ethnic, and ideological politics. The last is now losing much of its power as the demands for efficiency and new services become more vocal. But, the localism of the past, like the feudal guild system in the early era of industrial capitalism, remains important. As the suburbs challenge the hegemony of the cities and towns, the political economy of the state becomes wedded to that of the nation. The struggle for political power is influenced by the differing impact of the national political economy on the managerial classes and the industrial and town populations. This, in turn, explains the behavior of the rural and core-city legislators in the bastion of the General Court, and also explains the divergent concepts of state and party government that transcend party cleavages.

The people who are trying to override the old order on the crest of their prosperity and achievement are the new class of professionals, typified on the national level by politicians of both parties and on the local level by middle-class amateurs. The conflict is cultural, institutional, political, and social. Its outcome is likely to determine the ability of the Commonwealth to govern effectively.

PART I

POLITICAL TRANSITIONS: *THE BASES OF POWER*

Political systems evolve; they are not made. The character of political systems reflects the pattern of the heritage through which they are extruded into the present, as well as the insistent determinism of the environment.

V. O. Key, Jr.
American State Politics

CHAPTER ONE

THE FOUR CULTURES: CHARACTERISTICS AND IDEOLOGIES

The Patricians: The Myth of Public Service

The patricians, the professional and business strata of old-stock lineage, have withdrawn from the political arena where numbers, organization, and alternative sources of political finance are liquid assets. The old families are widely publicized for their social activities, but they are less visible in the gubernatorial campaign, the urban renewal project, and the deliberations of the state legislature. Although the political omnipotence of men of wealth and social prominence is largely past, the patrician influence in Massachusetts politics does still endure. No coterie of elders, rum-runners, or bankers dictates public policy, "but no group which has as many banking, business and political ties as the Massachusetts aristocracy is suddenly going to be without power."[1] When he was told of the political collapse of the Boston Brahmins before the onslaughts of James Michael Curley and his immigrant following, Cleveland Amory noted the presence of "Governor Robert P. Bradford of Mayflower ancestry, two Senators by the names of Leverett Saltonstall and Henry Cabot Lodge, and a battery of Coolidges, Cod-

[1] Duane Lockard, *New England State Politics* (Princeton: Princeton University Press, 1959), p. 119.

mans, Curtises, and Parkmans and Wigglesworths, all of whom had been extremely successful in the political line."[2] Nearly three decades later, there is still Senator Saltonstall, flanked by Endicott Peabody, of Mayflower descent, and George Cabot Lodge, a likely candidate for political office.

The relationship of this elite to the political system has nothing of the patroon's arrogance, the Southern Bourbon's paternalism, or the robber baron's divine right to exploit. The family firm merges with the national corporation, ownership is no longer managerial power, and the old barriers crumble before the new men. A nation which does not have an aristocratic past and has an eye on a self-made future will eschew the public notables of the past and shape new political elites which win deference through time, money, and inclination. The patricians' political interests do not usually run counter to the fiscal policies of State Street and the First National Bank, but neither are they equated simply with the economic interests of those institutions. The ability of the patricians to conserve political power despite a relative decline in their public resources is due rather to their capacity to absorb and accommodate the vagaries of the social structure.

Since 1930, the patricians' political efforts through the Republican Party have been directed toward public service, the recruitment of leaders, and the maintenance of political discipline in the tradition of Burke, Disraeli, and Harold Macmillan. They have provided gradual, flexible, competent party leadership similar to that of the British Conservative Party with which they have so much in common. Patricians such as Lodge, Herter, and Saltonstall have also comprised the basic leadership in the business and financial communities and have formed a part of the inner core of the Republican Party. Their power is based on high social status, fiscal and corporate wealth, and skills in leadership derived from

2 Cleveland Amory, *The Proper Bostonians* (New York: Dutton, 1947), p. 345.

education and training that have been made possible by these advantages. The typical patrician is likely to be a Protestant of a high-status denomination (Episcopal or Congregational), a banking or insurance executive, and the resident of a suburb such as Lincoln, Bedford, Weston, or Chelmsford.

The patricians, as the top organizational managers, have considerable intercourse with the other segments of the owners, bankers, and rentiers. They are political brokers who mediate conflicts between individuals and subgroups, between the private and the public realms, and between the creditors of the paper economy and the debtors of the consumption-oriented middle class. This is not the *ancien régime*, oblivious to changes in a democratic and restless society. The patricians, like their Puritan forefathers, strive to carry out the handiwork of God with a modest profit, a balanced budget, and an account of social debts to be paid in full.

This orientation leads to investment in tomorrow rather than withdrawal from the accomplishments of the past. When a space-age corporation is formed, designed to boost the economy of the state with more government contracts, the board of trustees includes Lloyd D. Brace, Chairman of the First National Bank of Boston; Erskine White, President of the New England Telephone & Telegraph Company; Bryon K. Elliott, President of the John Hancock Mutual Life Insurance Company; O. Kelley Anderson, President of the New England Mutual Life Insurance Company; William Webster, President of Yankee Atomic Energy Company; and Erwin D. Canham, Editor of *The Christian Science Monitor* and the Chairman of the Federal Reserve Bank of Boston.

Just as, in Calvin's Geneva, Tawney's England, and Winthrop's Bay Colony, the elders planned for tomorrow's public economy with the resources of today's prestige and power, so today the patricians are the brokers in the changeover from a mass industrial society, symbolized by the automobile, to a postindustrial scientific technocracy, symbolized by space research and by highly skilled personnel.[3]

This elite exercises large measures of private decision-making power. Radical change that would affect the power base, political position, and welfare of the patricians is opposed or moderated. As rightful governors who must increasingly share power with others if they are to sustain their own hegemony, the patricians need to participate actively in politics through a loyal hard core.

This hard core is found especially among the older Republican rank and file. For example, in Newton, formerly a Yankee Republican stronghold, the loyal party workers of the powerful local organization are elderly Yankees who are either retired or pensioned.[4] Demographic and political power changes, however, and the patricians no longer run the Republican Party. Party power is now often in the hands of younger revisionists from ethnic minority groups and political representatives of the yeomanry from sparsely populated areas who dominate the party ranks in the state legislature and in the town committees.

The patrician political style includes an interest in local, state, national, and international issues — it is cosmopolitan. The ancient rallying cry, "the best government governs least," is still heard in discussions of private initiative and federal spending at the Chamber of Commerce, the Somerset Club, and on the financial pages of the *Boston Herald* and *The Christian Science Monitor*. It coexists with and is supported

[3] See David T. Bazelon, "The Scarcity Makes," *Commentary, 34* (October 1962), 293–304; C. Wright Mills, *The Power Elite* (New York: Oxford University Press, 1956), pp. 147–170; and E. Digby Baltzell, *Philadelphia Gentlemen* (Glencoe, Ill.: The Free Press, 1958).

[4] David Rubenstein, "A Study of Voting Patterns in Newton, Massachusetts," unpublished MS, 1962. This sample survey also found that 52 per cent of the retired are registered Republicans, as against 39 per cent of those with professional occupations, and 27 per cent with proprietor-manager occupations when differences of age are held constant.

by an interest in civil liberties, civil rights, constitutional reform, and urban renewal and transportation measures designed to improve the political community. Of course, such measures also serve economic self-interest and hope for the alteration of industrial and residential patterns in the core city and its environs. Thus, the patricians oppose extreme political measures initiated by segments of the managerial elite (peace movements), the yeomen (favorable responses to the John Birch Society), or the workers and their political spokesmen (McCarthyism).

One aspect of the patrician hold on public life is its role in relating new political events to older patterns. If, as Richard Hoggart maintains, "the essence of working-class life . . . is the dense and concrete life, a life whose main stress is on the intimate, the sensory, the detailed, and the personal,"[5] then the enduring political hegemony of the patricians must be traced to their ability to link the personal and public spheres.

The patricians, as brokers of a changing economic society, mediate between the larger world of Washington and the confines of the town and the ward. Their links with the past and their confidence in mastering the future provide experience with which to meet the impact of international cartels, common markets, and automation on the home, the family, and the job. Since the social definitions of patrician status are not static, the Lodges, the Saltonstalls, and now the Kennedys, have honored claims on the political system's past, and their presence reinforces the confidence of those who are uncertain about its future.

The Yeomen: The Myth of the Past

The small towns fade from sight along the turnpikes, the farms go untilled, and the men of public affairs turn their

[5] Richard Hoggart, *The Uses of Literacy* (New York: Oxford University Press, 1957), p. 88.

attention from town and county government to the politics of the metropolis and of the suburbs. Members of a declining culture are not likely to have a mellow view of the world, especially when they have few skills that are marketable in a national political economy. When a suburban Republican representative chides his party's legislative floor manager because "he acts . . . like the moderator of a Town Meeting,"[6] the sanctity of older New England governmental structures is destroyed and the power of its architects is doomed.

The yeomen, who comprise the old-stock residue of small businessmen and rural workers, form the solid core of the Massachusetts Republican Party, and their views are reflected in the conservatism of the local weeklies, rather than the urbane, Boston Republican press. The prevailing ethos is that of nineteenth-century America with its emphasis on individual initiative, its distrust of bigness in government, corporations, labor unions, and international organizations, and a personalized, informal attitude toward friends and neighbors in the school committee, the bank, and the State House in Boston. The blue-collar population, even in the new-stock Italian and French towns, is likely to be less Democratic and less unionized than its counterpart in the cities. Moreover, the air of the company town hangs over the depopulated mill town suffering from the exodus to the South of textiles, shoes, and lasts.

This depleted power position of the yeomen reflects the general decline of small-town and rural areas in American economic and political life, a phase of American politics that has left lasting and often outmoded norms of political conduct.[7] Robert Wood has found that suburbs often "intensify

[6] The remark of a suburban Republican legislator about his party's small-town minority leader, quoted in *The Christian Science Monitor*, January 15, 1962, p. 2.

[7] See Arthur J. Vidich and Joseph Bensman, *Small Town in Mass Society* (Princeton: Princeton University Press, 1958); Andrew Hacker, "The Elected and the Anointed," *American Political Science*

and exaggerate the traditional politics of small localities. More completely nonpartisan than the one-party small towns in rural areas, and with the activities of the party leader more severely limited, the suburban municipalities represent the principle of direct popular participation in a mode theoretically workable under modern circumstances."[8]

However, the new managerial class in suburbia is more immersed in the politics of the larger world than the small-town yeomanry which preceded it. In fact, the yeoman ideology contains the seeds of its own destruction as the attendance at the town meeting decreases, the new residents win their battles for higher taxes and more schools, and civic leadership falls into younger hands.

Although, in a major American voting study, Campbell and his associates stress the social isolation of the farm and the small town to explain American rural voting behavior, the insularity of the yeomen's political behavior is probably accounted for by the destruction of traditional values.[9] Replaced by a young managerial stratum, bypassed by the industries, turnpikes, and shopping developments of a consumption-oriented society, the yeomen have lost their sense of usefulness, their participation in the mainstream of American life. Their political behavior seems archaic. In this "shiny new world" there is no place for the village store, the informality and folksiness of the town meeting, and the older mass media with a small-town orientation such as the *Saturday Evening Post*.[10]

The political consequences of these transitions are im-

Review, LV (September 1961), 539–549; and Robert C. Wood, *Suburbia* (Boston: Houghton Mifflin, 1959), pp. 91–134.

8 Wood, *op. cit.*, p. 195.

9 Angus Campbell, Phillip E. Converse, Warren E. Miller, and Donald E. Stokes, *The American Voter* (New York: Wiley, 1960), pp. 411–440.

10 Town meetings are sparsely attended. No more than 3 per cent of the registered voters attended any of the forty-seven annual town meetings reported in the Boston metropolitan press in 1962–1963.

portant. A significant study that was made among small-town businessmen found a strong distrust of modern industrial society, that is, opposition to corporations and labor unions, and support of Senator Joseph McCarthy.[11] This distrust also extended to civil liberties, constitutional reforms, and metropolitan planning proposals advanced by the professional and business classes of the cities.

The political ideology of the yeomen in Massachusetts includes an emphasis on moral corruption in Boston and other cities, and sporadic electoral participation in elections, which is characterized by outbursts of nativism, xenophobia, and rightist political movements.[12] It is no accident that four of the state senatorial districts where membership in the John Birch Society includes a majority of the adult population, are in towns with a population between ten and twenty thousand, an old-stock Yankee base, and a declining economy. Nor is it surprising that the two largest conservative newspapers in the state are published by old-stock Yankees in cities where political participation is low, there is considerable unemployment, and the educational levels are among the lowest in the state.[13]

The Yeomen "deprecate the present to acquire a vague sense of equality"[14] and restore the past. While they share the fiscal conservatism of the patricians, however, they lack the strategic social positions that unite the latter with the

[11] Martin Trow, "Small Businessmen, Political Tolerance, and Support for McCarthy," *American Journal of Sociology, LXIV* (1958), 275–280.

[12] The voting turnout of the yeomanry has fluctuated more than that of any other class. See J. Joseph Huthmacher, *Massachusetts People and Politics, 1919–1933* (Cambridge: Harvard University Press, 1959), pp. 272–278, and Chapter 8.

[13] Innovation in Massachusetts political communications is closely linked to the Boston and other metropolitan areas. The reactionary press of small towns and provincial cities is probably related to isolation from the centers of journalism and television.

[14] Eric Hoffer, *The True Believer* (New York: Harper and Brothers, 1951), p. 70.

new captains of science, administration, and technology. Their resistance to urban renewal, constitutional reform, and party reorganization stems from a lack of class consciousness that ordinarily allows small-town representatives to feel that they have some say in the new order.

There is little self-confident conservatism in Massachusetts because rural and small-town areas occupy little political space in an urbanized, industrialized, and increasingly Democratic state.[15] There are few articulate and statewide farm and fraternal groups to coalesce the yeomanry into a more effective political force. If the yeomen's political style is parochial, it is a fragmented parochialism. Each town has to cope alone with the suburban managerial advance.

This is the heritage of the town meeting and of the self-sufficient New England Yankee; interest is centered on local tax increases, property zoning, and the maintenance of restricted industrial and mercantile wealth. However, laissez-faire easily becomes mercantilism in the economic market place. Small-town officials, despite their political moralism, strongly opposed a conflict-of-interest law, in 1960, that prevented the town clerk or selectman from purchasing stationery supplies from his own shop or selling pharmaceutical supplies to the city from his drug store. Moreover, southern New England dairymen are not opposed to a federal subsidy of their Greater Boston market since it defeats the competitive advantages held by the dairymen of Vermont and New Hampshire.

The yeomen, selectmen, and state legislators often oppose the Boston-centered business and financial community — an opposition that extends to reforms in the Republican Party and greater fiscal support for education from the towns. For example, the small-town-dominated legislative wing of the

[15] See John H. Fenton, "Ohio's Unpredictable Voters," *Harper's*, *CCV* (October 1962), 61–65; Leon Epstein, "Size of Place and the Division of the Two-Party Vote in Wisconsin," *Western Political Quarterly*, *IX* (1956), 138–156.

Republican Party voted 69–37 against Governor Foster Furcolo's sales tax in 1957, although the measure received the support of the Republican state chairman, the leaders of the business community, and the *Boston Herald* and *Traveler*.[16] Five years later, in 1962, enough Republican legislators, most of them from medium-sized towns, supported Democratic Speaker John Thompson to allow him to regain his position after a six-ballot struggle against a Democratic governor, the party chairman, and significant metropolitan support in the lower chamber. The *Boston Herald-Traveler* and the State Street centers of Republican wealth castigated the party's legislative leadership for its obstruction of rational, moderate reform.

The yeomen, then, maintain a doctrine of religious and political hegemony that thrived at an earlier time. Their political frame of reference is not Edmund Burke but Ecclesiastes: "Is there anything whereof it may be said, See, this is new? It hath been already of old time which was before us."[17]

The Workers: The Myth of Solidarity

In August of 1922, a heated debate (between two pre-Stalinist Communist Party groups, the Geese and the Liquidators) over the future of American radicalism, centered on the Party's role in public relations in order to gain the support of the masses. In the sleepy town of Bridgeman, Michigan, however, these polemics merely roused the citizenry and resulted in the arrest of some of the group by governmental agents. In this comedy of errors even "the choice of Bridgeman was itself a gross miscalculation, for the Communists could have lost themselves more easily in a Manhattan cafe-

[16] John P. Mallan and George Blackwood, "The Tax That Beat a Governor: The Ordeal of Massachusetts," in *The Uses of Power*, edited by Alan F. Westin (New York: Harcourt, Brace and World, 1962), pp. 285–322.

[17] *Ecclesiastes* 1:10.

teria than in a village where the appearance of a stranger constituted news."[18] So it has been with socialism in America.

The workers, the new-stock, low-income groups of the major cities, are no longer viewed as the bulwark of American democracy. In the words of one writer, "It is not to 'The People,' not to the business class, not to the working class, that we must look for the consistent and relatively unqualified defense of freedom and equality."[19] Concomitantly, as the relative strength of the labor unions tapers off, the working-class core of Massachusetts democracy finds that it must share political power with the professional class. This transition follows shifts in the New England economy; shifts that indicate less the effects of manufacture than they do those of developments in research, aerospace, and electronics.[20]

Although it is no longer the political domain of the Irish and of the other immigrants who contributed so much to its fermentation, the Bay State and its majority party are still significantly affected by this cultural heritage. The election of 1928 forged the immigrant groups into a self-conscious coalition within the Democratic Party, a coalition that endured throughout the New Deal era. More recently, Catholic minority groups, especially the sensitive Italo-American population, have produced members of the political class that have fought for control of the workers' party. This alignment between the dominant Irish and the subordinate Italian, French, and Polish politicians is now less relevant, however, than the cleavage between the workers and the managerial leadership.

The workers, like the yeomen, share a limited range of political concern. They are localists, with a deep resistance to governmental, social, and economic change because they perceive, often correctly, that the strategies of constitutional

[18] Irving Howe and Lewis Coser, *The American Communist Party* (New York: Praeger, 1957), p. 99.

[19] Robert E. Lane, "The Fear of Equality," *American Political Science Review, XLVIII* (March 1959), 51.

[20] The Federal Reserve Bank of Boston, *Annual Report*, 1962.

reform and urban renewal threaten their entrenched positions in the neighborhood, the legislature, and the Executive Council — an eight-member body, elected from large districts, that advances local interests through its statutory powers to approve appointments of the governor in the executive branch of the government.

The urban core is essentially Populist because its political ideology is based on that of the immigrants, and friends and neighbors in the ward or parish. Democratic Party loyalty, however, is strong, especially among the Irish Catholics since the party is largely theirs and manifests the cultural characteristics of its dominant supporters.

The workers share the managers' view toward social welfare — they favor labor power over corporate hegemony. Unlike the suburban wing of the party, the workers traditionally manifest little support for civil rights, foreign economic aid, civil liberties, constitutional reform, and urban renewal.[21] This political orientation is anchored in social, ethnic, occupational, and religious roots, and in a continuing sense of being the underdog.

It is their political style as underdogs that warrants the most attention. The essence of this style is solidarity. It is not the solidarity of Marxist theorists, for it is less class conscious than class resistant; it is, rather, the intricate pattern of familial, social, and ethnic relationships that strikes reformers. A student of the English working class concludes that "the more we look at working-class life, the more we try to reach the core of working-class attitudes, the more

[21] See Chapter 4, "Working-Class Authoritarianism," in Seymour M. Lipset, *Political Man* (Garden City, N.Y.: Doubleday, 1959), pp. 97–130; Lane, *op. cit.;* Christian Bay, *The Structure of Freedom*, (Stanford: Stanford University Press, 1958), pp. 240–312; Edward Shills, *The Torments of Secrecy* (Glencoe, Ill.: The Free Press, 1956); Martin Meyerson and Edward C. Banfield, *Politics, Planning and the Public Interest* (Glencoe, Ill.: The Free Press, 1955), pp. 91–120; Peter H. Rossi and Robert A. Dentler, *The Politics of Urban Renewal* (New York: The Free Press of Glencoe, 1963).

surely does it appear that that core is a sense of the personal, the concrete, the local: it is embodied in the idea of, first, the family, and, second, the neighborhood."[22]

The strength of group identification is probably weaker in Dorchester and South Boston than in London's East End and the Liverpool Central Exchange. Nevertheless, in each case, there is the sense of creating a niche within the system; and its maintenance demands unity against the intrusion of those who would alter it. For instance, old-line Democrats passively resist the call to reform of an eager young gubernatorial candidate by not hearing his pleas for party support. A veteran congressman, whose task has been to reach the urban core, has clearly described this pattern of loyalties and political responses:

> There isn't any political boss in a city like Boston. In Chicago, you call Daley and something will happen. Here you have to carefully consult the right people in each ward and section. There are established customs and territories. These cannot be breached. Also, you have to approach these people in the proper way. They want to feel important, and they are important. You don't read them the riot act or start yelling about principles. You start by asking how their wives and kids are and this isn't just to butter them up. You do it because you care and because they are important. In fact, you could say politics in this city are built on these personal relations or they are built on sand.

The urban core tend their personal affairs and give public trusteeship to their elective and union officials until politics trespasses on their personal, concrete world. When urban renewal comes to the home and the street, and when constitutional reform brings a vacant chair in the office of the ward representative, then the workers pay attention to the ascending managerial class that may have been responsible for the redevelopment and the reapportionment.

[22] Hoggart, *op. cit.*, p. 32.

The Managers: The Myth of Rational Progress

In Massachusetts, the basic culture can be observed of the administrative state and of the growing managerial strata that occupy the sprawling metropolitan fringes. An authoritative report informs New England manufacturers that they "typically use less capital per worker and have been investing less per worker in capital facilities than their national counterparts,"[23] yet Massachusetts now ranks third in the dollar value of its military contracts; its per capita income has risen 52 per cent in the last decade, slightly more than for the nation as a whole; and space and aeronautics research contracts are being pushed in Washington and on Beacon Hill. The National Planning Association expects a 103 per cent increase in personal income, and a 50 per cent boost in nonmanufacturing employment, except agriculture, over the next two decades, while at the same time it expects an increase of only 35 per cent in population, 34 per cent in the total labor force, and 20 per cent in manufacturing.

While the managers, the high-income, professional-technical class of increasingly new-stock heritage, share or exceed the skills of the patricians, they do not have their wealth, social status, or corporate power. The managers are products of two revolutions: the economic revolution that broke the bonds between ownership and power, and the political revolution of the New Deal and the Fair Deal that provided access for the offspring of immigrants to the professional, scientific, technical, and administrative positions in society. As a group so young, the managers have no one political tradition. Indeed, their tradition is a composite of their heritage and their aspirations. The heritage is Democratic, urban, immigrant, blue-collar, and entrepreneurial; the aspirations are for "status," defined as upper-class, patrician Protestantism, and Republican Party membership.

Two factors, however, have changed their perspectives.

[23] The Federal Reserve Bank of Boston, *op. cit.*

One has been the invigoration and high status that Kennedy has given to the Democratic Party membership, a phenomenon most meaningful to the Catholics among the managerial intellectuals; the other has been the new prestige of professional skills over that of social background.

David Bazelon summarizes these transitions in status, and the characteristics of the managerial or administrative intellectuals when he writes:

> The Intellectuals in question are avant-garde only in spearheading a social revolution; they are not avant-garde in the usual sense, meaning culturally advanced, highbrow, or disaffected. They are Intellectuals in that they . . . *use systematic concepts in their productive, earning-a-living work, and it is necessary that they be trained to do this, which distinguishes them from those who have not received such training.* The training, or education, is a new form of income-producing status which replaces and serves the same function as the older bourgeois ownership of income-producing property.[24]

The typical managers have middle-class status, are either Jewish, Yankee, or Irish, and live in the inner suburbs of the Boston and Springfield metropolitan areas (Newton, Arlington, Westfield). Since they are administrators and free professionals (clergymen, teachers, lawyers), their emphasis is on the rational ordering of the environment. These political activists increasingly include scientists and technicians in electronics, aerospace, advertising, and communications. Managerial politics is thus different from the earlier Progressive movement that had a more limited social base in the free professions of law, teaching, and the ministry.[25] It is no wonder, then, that the managerial ascendancy has become a matter of political concern:

[24] Bazelon, *op. cit.*, p. 300. © Copyright 1962 by David T. Bazelon. Reprinted from *The Paper Economy*, by David T. Bazelon, by permission of Random House, Inc.

[25] See Richard Hofstadter, *The Age of Reform* (New York: Knopf, 1955), pp. 138–173.

> This is the age of the managers, and what is needed is a way to civilize them. Introducing them to the pleasures of being gentlemen and scholars in their off hours may be helpful in this task, but such training hardly strikes at the heart of the matter, and neither does a course in Plato. . . .They must learn somehow to relate both pressing and long-term human problems to the kind of seemingly abstract decisions they will be called upon to make.[26]

The managers are in favor of constitutional reform and increased aid to private and public education. Because they are cosmopolitan they are the least class-conscious and the least party-bound group. Because they have high educational and occupational attainments their political emphasis is on merit rather than personalized reward. They have a penchant for rational criteria in government. They are the least likely to respond to ethnoreligious appeals, for example, and they form an electorate that is more concerned with policy than patronage, charisma, and the politics of revenge.

The managers share the patricians' liberality over civil liberties, civil rights, constitutional reform, and urban renewal; they believe in equal opportunities — perhaps more so than the patricians. The latter strive to retain what power remains and so avoid becoming a "natural aristocracy in this country, a sort of powerless elite who, though shunted aside first by Jacksonian democracy, then by the proprietors of the industrial revolution, retained control of many of our oldest and finest cultural institutions which were consolation prizes for them as losers in the big power game."[27] On the other hand, the managers share the concern of the workers for social and economic welfare measures and, in the past, they reacted more favorably to labor than to the demands of corporate power. They do not disdain either major economic institution because they are mobile men; and their progress

26 Richard Schickel, "Soft Advice, Hard Problems" (a review of August Heckscher, *The Public Happiness*), *Commentary*, *34* (October 1962), 357.

27 *Ibid.*, p. 355.

across the frontiers of research, education, and communications may buttress the equalitarianism that Frederick Jackson Turner saw in the old frontier of land and social space.

However, as the managers acquire power, their equalitarianism may diminish. Indeed, "the Intellectuals (managers) and the Politicians (patricians) are increasingly engaged in an intra-class struggle. The former want, simply, to be less managed by the latter; or, they want a fuller realization and development of the new managerial order — which means an increase in their own power and status — and they want it sooner rather than later."[28] The achievement of these desires may adversely affect the managers' support of both civil liberties for unpopular minorities and of civil rights for the nonmanagerial classes.

Indeed, an increase in power, accompanied by conservative fears of mass movements in a changing political economy, may erode the heritage of progressive reform. The "left wing" of the managerial group may be traced to the heritage of Stevenson, with a further splintering off into the "peace movement." The "right-wing" antecedents of conservative, accepted power may lead to increased strength for respectable candidates with these views — the Goldwaters, not the McCarthys. The middle path of managerial politics is perhaps illustrated by COD, the Democratic reform group in Massachusetts, with its careful selection of qualified candidates in the inner suburbs, and an organizational structure in which the leadership was predominantly Irish Catholic and the core membership was Yankee-Jewish.

In Table 1.1 the major characteristics of the yeomen, the workers, the managers, and the patricians are summarized. Most of these points have been developed in this chapter. The classification of "issue-orientation" hinges on the extent to which politics is judged within the context of political ideas: at one extreme are ideological response sets and at

[28] Bazelon, *op. cit.*, p. 301.

TABLE 1.1
MASSACHUSETTS POLITICAL STRATA AND THEIR CHARACTERISTICS

Dominant Characteristics	*Patrician Elite (Patricians)*	*Managerial Intellectuals (Managers)*	*Urban Workers (Workers)*	*Small Town, Rural, Business, Labor (Yeomen)*
Party Affiliation	Republican	Mixed to Democratic	Democratic	Republican
Residence	Outer suburbs	Inner suburbs	Core cities	Small towns
Power base	Wealth, Skill	Skill	Numbers	Numbers
Social Class	Upper	Upper-middle	Lower-middle, Working	Lower-middle, Working
Ethnicity	Old-stock Yankee	New-stock Jewish, Irish	New-stock Italian, Irish	Old-stock Yankee
Religion	Protestant	Mixed	Catholic	Protestant
Occupation	Finance, Business	Administrative, Technical	Blue-collar	Entrepreneurial, Blue-collar
Power Position	Contracting	Expanding	Slightly contracting	Substantially contracting
Political Style	Cosmopolitan	Cosmopolitan	Parochial	Parochial
Attitude toward Change	Conservative	Progressive	Conservative	Reactionary
Political Ideology	Elitist	Elitist, Equalitarian	Populist	Bargaining, Town meeting
Issue-Orientation	Ideological	Ideological, Group benefits	Group-benefits, Nature of times	Nature of times, Personalities of candidates
Party Loyalty	Moderately strong	Weak	Moderately strong	Strong
Attitude toward Social Welfare	Conservative	Liberal	Liberal	Conservative
Attitude toward Civil Liberties, Rights, Urban Renewal	Liberal	Liberal	Conservative	Conservative
Attitude toward Unions, Corporations	Accept both but favor corporations	Organization men, accept both	Accept both but favor unions	Anti-organization men, accept neither
Attitude toward Party, Governmental reor-	Somewhat favorable	Very favorable	Very unfavorable	Very unfavorable

the other are transitory choices that alter with the immediate conditions of life and the personalities of the candidates. Judgments on the basis of the benefits to be derived from one's salient political group membership come between these two poles. This cultural perspective provides a powerful and broad guideline for the political analysis of Massachusetts government. The first step in that analysis is a review of electoral behavior in four critical gubernatorial elections that have strongly influenced the state's political history. An assessment will be made, in Chapter 2, of the relationships between the cultural characteristics and the political behavior of the four major social groupings in these elections.

CHAPTER TWO

COALITIONS AND CRITICAL ELECTIONS: THE CHANGING MANDATES

"The Standing Order": 1920–1930

There are few tragedies that exceed that of Woodrow Wilson dying, brokenhearted on the bier of the Fourteen Points, which were to gird the League of Nations founded on the rule of law and open covenants. There are, moreover, few elections more indicative of the collapse of party than that of 1920 in Massachusetts and throughout the nation.

Wilson's successor as party chief, James M. Cox, was soundly beaten by the Republican orthodoxy of Warren G. Harding; and the Democratic share of the presidential vote declined 19.1 per cent from its level at Wilson's election in 1916. In the gubernatorial contest in Massachusetts, the Republican Channing Cox defeated the Wilsonite, John Jackson Walsh, by more than a two-to-one margin; and the G.O.P. maintained its grip on all other constitutional offices in the state. The four-man Democratic Congressional minority was halved as Wilson's supporters went down in defeat. In the 280-member General Court, the Democratic minority was pared by more than 20 per cent. On the eve of the election, the Democratic State Chairman, Michael O'Leary, made a terse statement: "The first hundred years are the hardest. Martin Lomasney will be elected to the House from Ward Five."[1]

The politics of postwar disillusionment retarded for a decade the growth of two-party competitiveness, which had previously enabled the Democratic minority to thrive. The party that had elected the first Irish Catholic to state office and the first Democratic U.S. senator since the Civil War, and had contributed to Wilson's victories in 1912 and 1916, had suffered a devastating defeat. The misnamed "Age of Normalcy" had begun; and the lack of harmony and security among immigrant Democrats in Massachusetts was to fragment the party until the critical presidential election of 1928 and the gubernatorial victory of 1930.[2]

It was the isolationist, xenophobic, and ethnic antagonism toward Wilson's policies that assured the domination of the Republican Party. These policies brought dissension among the major social strata in the Commonwealth, the old-stock Yankees and the others of northern-European extraction, the Irish Americans, and the mélange of "newer races" from southern and eastern Europe. The postwar yearning for relaxation and a reduction in governmental controls had

[1] Quoted in J. Joseph Huthmacher, *Massachusetts People and Politics, 1919–1933* (Cambridge: Harvard University Press, 1959), p. 42. I have leaned heavily on this excellent study of interwar politics for basic data on the 1920, 1928, and 1930 gubernatorial elections. Material on the Dever setback of 1952 is more fragmentary, although James M. Burns, *John Kennedy: A Political Profile* (New York: Harcourt, Brace and World, 1959) provides useful insights into the political setting of the time. I have relied on personal observation and participation in the 1962 contest for my analysis of the Peabody victory.

[2] I use the term "critical election" in two senses. I use it to mean a contest in which there is a significant realignment of major voting groups, and also one in which the prizes following the election are highly valued by at least one major stratum. See the theoretical statement of V. O. Key, Jr., "A Theory of Critical Elections," *The Journal of Politics, 17* (1955), 1–18; and its application in another state political system by Duncan MacRae, Jr., and James A. Meldrum, "Critical Elections in Illinois: 1888–1958," *American Political Science Review, LIV* (September 1960), 669–683.

specific appeal to the progressive and Democratic Yankees, but also produced an intense reaction to the nationalistic sentiments of the Irish, Italians, and other ethnic Americans. The cries of betrayal in response to the manipulations of postwar determinations of homeland sovereignty echoed from the hyphenated Americans and their organizations to the benefit of the "outs." "What did England get from the war?" a Republican orator asked an Irish-American audience in Springfield. "Everything in sight as usual."[3]

The organization of the Massachusetts Democratic Party collapsed. Five thousand fewer Democratic voters participated in the party's primary in 1920 than in 1916, despite the potential doubling of the electorate through the adoption of women's suffrage. John Jackson Walsh of Boston, a relatively unknown, pro-Wilson state senator, received the gubernatorial nomination in the absence of an organization candidate. There were no Democratic candidates for lieutenant governor, secretary of state, two Congressional seats, and numerous lesser offices. The Democratic Party nominated no candidates at all in 45.6 per cent of the state and county elective contests. With the notable exception of the Wilsonian progressives in academic and professional ranks, there was even little effort to organize the vote or debate the issues in Democratic councils. "The Massachusetts Irish, the backbone of the party, had literally gone on strike. The voices of their spellbinders, Walsh, Curley, Fitzgerald, and the rest were silent."[4]

Although the relative decline in the percentage of the Democratic vote did not vary significantly from one area to another, two new factors did affect the outcome: the advent of women's suffrage, which benefited Republican candidates because immigrant-derived norms did not include a political role for women, and the passive resistance of potential party adherents to the Wilsonian policies and candidates.

[3] Huthmacher, *op. cit.,* p. 37
[4] *Ibid.,* p. 33

In Boston's polyglot Ward 5, the domain of politically powerful Martin Lomasney, there was only a 12.6 per cent increase in registration compared with 65.5 per cent in Boston as a whole, 86.9 per cent in the thirty-eight other cities, and 92.1 per cent in the predominantly old-stock and Republican towns. League of Nations politics in the context of League of Nations foreign policy had fragmented the Massachusetts Democrats.

Two compilations of electoral data point to even greater consequences of the 1920 elections for the state's political system and for the four major cultural groupings that had shaped it. Although the gubernatorial candidate, Walsh, was drowned with James Cox in the anti-Wilson tide, he did run ahead of the party's presidential candidate. There was, in addition, a positive correlation between the location, modified of course by the ethnicity of the Democratic vote, and Walsh's margin over Cox. With the notable exception of Boston where the "Irish Question" burned fiercely, Walsh's margin over his presidential running mate was greatest in the urban, ethnic, Democratic cities, and least in the old-stock Republican small towns. These differences were not due merely to organization or to the candidate himself, for Walsh waged an uninspiring campaign with a minimum of party organizational backing. Rather, they were due to an economic decline that aided the Democratic gubernatorial candidate: the proportion of unemployed union members rose from 8.7 per cent at the end of March 1920, to 31.8 per cent by December 31.

The Republican nostrum of economic orthodoxy — a belief in the invisible hand of the market aided by protective tariffs — reduced political losses due to a sagging economy, yet there was a gap in presidential and gubernatorial voting in ethnic, working-class Democratic cities, as shown in Table 2.1, a gap that reflected the economic basis to Democratic Party loyalty and the cohesiveness, by contrast, of the Republican hard-core electorate in the old-stock towns. The

TABLE 2.1

WALSH'S MARGIN OVER COX IN 1920: BY ETHNICITY, PLACE, AND CULTURAL BASE

	Percentage Difference
Ethnicity and Place:	
Boston	2.6
Ethnic Cities	5.5
Old-Stock Cities	3.9
Ethnic Places	3.4
Old-Stock Places	1.4
Ethnic Towns	0.6
Old-Stock Towns	–0.8
Cultural Base:	
Workers	4.6
Managers	3.6
Patricians	1.0
Yeomen	–0.4

Source: J. Joseph Huthmacher, *Massachusetts People and Politics, 1919–1933* (Harvard University Press, 1959), pp. 277–278.

variation in the gubernatorial vote manifested a party cleavage between the core of the Democratic workers and the Republican yeomen on basic economic issues that has provided an enduring basis for party conflict.

The Democratic debacle of 1920 was a manifestation of tensions which resulted from foreign policy, isolationism and its effects, and ethnic rivalries. Most of all, the election expressed the marginal feeling of the immigrant Americans in the face of old European loyalties and new American hostilities.

The old-stock reaction to Irish, Italian, and Syrian demands for self-determination took several forms. First, there was the self-protective association of the Loyal Coalition, formed by prominent old-stock Bostonians and Northern Irish loyalists to combat the propaganda of De Valera, the Sinn Fein, and their American sympathizers. Its message was simple and impassioned: "If you are a good American, desire good government . . . keep the hyphenates out of American public affairs. . . ."[5] Second, political candidates did not always restrain their private feelings in discussions of newer Americans and their volatile politics. Governor Cox, in the swirl of clamorous demands from the ethnic groups, bitterly condemned Italian, Greek, and other ethnic factions which backed Harding as a "motley array of questionable groups and influences . . . an array that to survey brings the crimson blush of humiliation to an American."[6] He castigated "the Afro-American party, whose hyphenated activity has attempted to stir up troubles among Negroes upon false claims that it can bring social equality."[7] Even more grating to the identity and esteem of those suffering conflict between the familiar patterns of the old world and the uncertainty of the new, were the sober judgments of a Princeton academician:

> But now there came multitudes of men of the lower class from the south of Italy and men of the meanest sort out of Hungary and Poland, men out of the ranks where there was neither skill nor energy nor any initiative of quick intelligence; and they came in numbers that increased from year to year, as if the countries of the South of Europe were disburdening themselves of the more sordid and hapless elements of the population.[8]

It was one thing for the man, torn between Sicily and East Boston or Dorchester and County Cork, to oppose the Klan, the Yankee factory owner, and the Loyal Coalition; it was another for him to contest the words of an eminent political scientist who was to become the distinguished President, Woodrow Wilson.

The election of 1920 was critical because it was a crisis of political identity for the prevailing political and cultural structure of the state and nation. The Irish and the newer

5 *Ibid.*, p. 27.
6 *Ibid.*, p. 32.
7 *Ibid.*, p. 32.
8 *Ibid.*, p. 27.

Americans, responding to the nationalist aspirations of their homelands, found themselves alienated from the major symbols that linked an individual to his government, such as civic duty, Protestantism, and nativism. They were outsiders to a closed political system. Even the Massachusetts Democratic Party ignored the claims of Irish and Italian rights in the old country as well as in the new. The Democratic gubernatorial vote in 1920, shown in Table 2.2, indicated the relationship between cultural and party predilections. The failure of the Democrats to carry Boston, the party's bastion, underscored the political force of ethnic grievances and the weakness of ethnic-party loyalties.

TABLE 2.2
DEMOCRATIC GUBERNATORIAL VOTE IN 1920: BY ETHNICITY, PLACE, AND CULTURAL BASE

	Democratic Percentage of Total Vote
Ethnicity and Place:	
Boston	42.3
Ethnic Cities	36.4
Old-Stock Cities	27.8
Ethnic Places	36.7
Old-Stock Places	22.9
Ethnic Towns	34.0
Old-Stock Towns	20.2
Cultural Base:	
Workers	39.5
Managers	34.4
Patricians	27.9
Yeomen	21.3

Source: Based on data in J. Joseph Huthmacher, *Massachusetts People and Politics, 1919–1933,* p. 278.

The historical facts are understandable. Ethnic resentments took their toll of Democratic votes in the workers' urban centers. Warren G. Harding's brand of jovial Rotarian Republicanism represented admirably the ideology of the small-town yeomanry, but, on the other hand, the managerial and patrician cultures included a body of Wilsonian internationalists, drawn from the academies and professions, who were represented by Winthrop Murray Crane and the *Springfield Republican.*

The relationship between voting behavior and the cultural base is meaningful only in the context of the specific issues that shaped the 1920 campaign: xenophobia, isolationism, and ethnic nationalism. Indeed, the data in Table 2.3 supports the attribution, in the preceding chapter, of dominant characteristics to each political culture. *The volatility, but not the rate of participation of the yeomen-worker strata, is greatest when issues involving basic identification with the political system are in controversy.*

TABLE 2.3

DECLINE IN DEMOCRATIC PRESIDENTIAL VOTE, 1916–1920: BY ETHNICITY, PLACE, AND CULTURAL BASE

	Percentage Decline
Ethnicity and Place:	
Boston	20.5
Ethnic Cities	20.4
Old-Stock Cities	18.0
Ethnic Places	15.7
Ethnic Towns	15.1
Old-Stock Places	18.7
Old-Stock Towns	19.0
Cultural Base:	
Workers	20.5
Managers	15.3
Patricians	18.3
Yeomen	18.9

Source: J. Joseph Huthmacher, *Massachusetts People and Politics, 1919–1933,* p. 278.

The Immigrant Uprising: 1928–1930

A political culture, to be viable, must have public symbols. By the mid-twenties, the patricians had supplied symbols in Lodge, Crane, Hoar, and Coolidge; and the yeomen had also furnished local leaders in state politics. The managerial stratum could look back upon its days of glory in the progressive era and ahead to its re-emergence in the fifties. If the urban working class had not had an Al Smith, they would surely have invented a similar cultural hero. The critical election of 1928 laid the foundation for the New Deal era of Franklin D. Roosevelt, for major shifts of power within the American government and the economy, and for the emergence of the national and Massachusetts Democrats as the majority party. The year 1928 was a landmark in a political crisis of integration.

In 1930, Joseph Ely became the first Democratic governor of Massachusetts since World War I. Before this gubernatorial takeover, there had already been the Al Smith revolution, and the Democratic revolution of David I. Walsh. Walsh, the first Irish Catholic to become a governor and U.S. senator, symbolized the achievement of political recognition. He also laid the groundwork for the party organization and recruitment that got started by the end of the twenties.

The history of Al Smith's nomination and the 1928 presidential campaign is quite familiar, and its impact on the Massachusetts political system will, therefore, be considered here.

In 1920, the Democratic Party had dwindled to an inactive shell that lacked resources. The campaigns of 1928 and 1930, however, saw the re-emergence of an articulate and relatively well-organized cadre ready to mobilize the party's traditional followers and reinforce the zeal of new converts.

The state executive committee was revived under the direction of Senator Walsh and State Chairman Frank Donoghue. The triumvirate of Walsh, Donoghue, and Ely also formed active ward and city committees and revitalized old defunct organizations. They formed ethnic political groups headed by young, ambitious, status-seeking members of the newer groups, registered new voters, channeled the now abundant flow of money, and campaigned vigorously for the alter ego of the newer, urban Americans like the governor of New York. The growing, and later disastrous, rift in party ranks between the Walsh-Ely coalition and the vociferous James Michael Curley was already evident in their attempts to outdo each other in mustering support for the "Happy Warrior," Al Smith. A keen student of interwar politics in Massachusetts states that "never before had so many aspiring politicians worked so hard for a Democratic presidential victory in Massachusetts."[9]

The upsurge in organizational activity produced reactions from a united and vigorous Republican Party that had a heritage of discipline in dispensing patronage within the state. In fact, the fierce campaign of 1928 solidified all party organizations, added almost 330,000 names to the registration lists as compared with 1924, and achieved a record vote of 93.5 per cent of all those registered.

In 1930, while the unity of the Republican Party was disrupted by Prohibition, the Democrats were discomfited by success. Curley, strongly aided in his quest for a third term as Mayor of Boston by the unity of his party support, backed "Honey Fitz" Fitzgerald against Joseph Ely in the gubernatorial convention; only the former's withdrawal because of illness saved the party from the embarrassment of dumping the convention-endorsed candidate. Although Fitzgerald's name remained on the primary ballot because of Curley's efforts and his own gubernatorial ambitions in 1932, Ely won by a two-to-one margin. There were four candidates for the

[9] *Ibid.*, p. 178.

party's senatorial nomination; but the timely support of Senator Walsh cleared the way for the nomination and eventual election of Marcus Coolidge. This leadership and enthusiasm maintained party cohesion into the nineteen thirties. Three organization-supported Yankee Democrats held the top positions on the Democratic slate for the last time in 1930. It was another three decades before a Democratic Protestant again headed the state ticket and received relatively united support from the party's rank and file.

The political contests of 1928 and 1930 differed considerably from that of 1920. In 1920, the central theme was identification with the symbols of American government, an identification that often conflicted, among the ethnic groups, with concern for the homeland. In 1928, the central theme was the integration of the political structure, as the marginal political man moved out of the ghetto into the larger political world. "For the first time," said a *New Republic* editorial, "a representative of the unpedigreed, foreign-born, city-bred, many-tongued recent arrivals on the American scene had knocked on the door and aspired seriously to the presiding seat in the national Chamber of Commerce."[10] The politics of recognition, power, and social mobility within the system was having its major contest.

It is important to add a second distinguishing characteristic of the political junctures of 1928 and 1930. Both elections involved critical appraisal of the government's role in the economy. It is only by considering this factor that one can account for the height of the Democratic tide each time, and the increase in strength of the Massachusetts Democrats in the 1930 gubernatorial contest when Al Smith was not on the ballot. Smith's campaign speeches on economic conditions, prosperity, and the tariff were underlined by the declining economic situation. Employment fell 10 per cent,

[10] *New Republic, L* (March 1927), 128.

and the value of manufactured goods decreased 6 per cent between 1926 and 1928.

Conditions were especially severe in the textile and industrial cities. In New Bedford, for example, employment dropped 30 per cent and the value of manufactured products 31 per cent. It was no wonder that New Bedford, along with Fall River, Lawrence, Lowell, Holyoke, and other cities which felt the economic deprivation, registered a strong swing to Smith in 1928. While the scarcity of economic and psychic income reinforced each other, the strong desire for recognition and political integration was also shown by the fact that the largest increase in the Democratic percentage of the presidential vote in Massachusetts occurred in the Franco-Polish city of Chicopee, where employment and payroll trends had actually improved since 1926. Relative deprivation rather than the gloom of absolute scarcity is a salient motive for political activity in democratic systems.

The tremors of the stock market crash of October 1929 helped the Democrats to recapture the governor's chair for the first time in fifteen years. Ely's victory in 1930 came in the midst of rapid falls in production, sales, and employment, after a campaign that supported two of the prime heresies of economic orthodoxy — deficit financing, and an unbalanced budget.

"I'd like to know why the credit of the State wasn't resorted to some months ago, and roads and buildings built," Ely demanded of Governor Fuller during the campaign, "as a means of helping the present critical unemployment situation."[11] Criticism of governmental economic policies merged with ethnic demands for political recognition by Democratic Party voters.

The shifting mandate of the four cultures can be charted between the gubernatorial contests of 1920 and 1930. The

[11] Quoted in Huthmacher, *op. cit.*, p. 211.

urban worker had become the heart of the Democratic Party, a fact that shaped the party's politics for two decades. The success of the Democrats in the decade after the 1920 debacle was least in the old-stock Yankee towns, the rock of Massachusetts Republicanism, while their gubernatorial advances were greatest in the urbanized centers, especially those with sizable foreign-stock elements.

It is important to note that Ely made sharp gains in cities with large ethnic, although not necessarily Irish, populations. Indeed, he secured a slightly greater share of the two-party vote in the state than had Al Smith in the 1928 presidential election. Although the western Massachusetts Yankee performed somewhat more poorly than Smith in new immigrant areas, he received 83.6 per cent of the vote in the predominantly Irish Ward 8 in Boston, the home of Mayor Curley's Tammany Club.

In the city of Boston, Ely ran 0.6 per cent ahead of Smith. He also gained some yeoman support on the basis of an ethnic, religious, and regional appeal, and ran 2.9 per cent ahead of Smith in the old-stock towns. Over the decade, however, the yeomanry resisted the Democratic trend.

The managerial strata united their progressive heritage with the philosophy of the incipient New Deal to give strong support to the Democratic advance; the patricians, however, showed considerably less attraction, over the decade, toward the ascending political party. In fact, high-status Yankee areas contributed a greater share of their vote to Smith than to Ely, for while the former was a product of New York's East Side, the latter talked the radicalism of deficit financing and unbalanced budgets. Among the "first families" of the Commonwealth, economic investments were more seriously considered than implicit threats to social status.

Urban political participation increased alongside the Democratic advance. The percentage of registrants who voted in the cities in 1930 was greater than in 1926, the previous "off-year" election, while in the towns it slightly declined. Consequently, we can say that *the volatility and rate of participation of the urban workers are high in critical elections involving demands for more political positions and an increased output in the allocation of economic values.*

"It is inevitable," wrote a Republican editor, "that, with the influences of 1928 at work, a great many persons who have been Republicans should have gone for a little outing behind the Democratic donkey."[12] This "little outing" was to last twenty-four years for presidential elections and nine years for gubernatorial elections. The demands of the urbanized immigrants and the glaring inconsistencies in the Republican talk of prosperity had revitalized and expanded the Democratic Party. A period of intense two-party competition was at hand in the state, and the party of Lodge, Coolidge, and Harding was soon to survey the political landscape from the position of the loyal minority opposition.

All the Last Hurrahs: 1952

Incessant inner-party friction and the weakening of the New Deal coalition through the intrusions of foreign policy weakened the Democratic Party's hegemony in the Commonwealth. In the seven elections preceding the gubernatorial contest of 1952, power rapidly changed hands. Four of these elections were won by Republicans (1938, 1940, 1942, 1946) and three by Democrats (1944, 1948, 1950).

This cyclical pattern can be contrasted with the four-term dominance of Democratic governors in the period 1930–1938. The average number of nominees for each statewide elective office increased from 6.4 in the period 1932–1940, to 6.8 in the period 1942–1952. The increasing activity and power of Curley, and of the party's Boston wing, was reflected in an increase, from 65.6 per cent to 82.9 per cent,

[12] *Boston Herald,* November 7, 1928, p. 10.

in the proportion of all the nominees who came from Boston and its vicinity during the two decades, and in an increase in the number of primary contests, even though "the division of the Democratic vote between Boston and vicinity and the rest of the state remained fairly constant."[13]

Despite these factors, the Democratic Party remained the normal majority party within the Massachusetts political system. It carried the state for its gubernatorial candidate in 64 per cent of the biennial elections from 1930 through 1962; and during that period, no Republican presidential candidate received more than 48 per cent of the vote — the share Hoover received in 1932. The state's lower house had its first Democratic majority in 1948. In the same year, the party elected half the members to the upper chamber, thereby breaking the G.O.P. monopoly in the Senate.

Nor were these the only Democratic gains. By 1954, Democratic Congressional representation equaled that of the Republicans in the House of Representatives. In 1948, for the first time since the Civil War, a Democrat served as secretary of state, and the party also held all of the other statewide constitutional offices. The Democratic gubernatorial loss in 1952 was, therefore, more than a temporary setback to the majority party. It implied basic changes in the cultural framework and the coalitions on which the parties had existed since Al Smith's presidential bid.

In 1952, Paul Dever, an Irish-American Democrat, lost the gubernatorial election to Christian Herter, a Yankee-Protestant Republican. It is difficult to contend that Christian Herter's success was due primarily to Dwight Eisenhower's presidential magnetism: although all state elections are susceptible to national influences, Massachusetts politics has produced noticeable variations when national and state contests are held simultaneously. John F. Kennedy, for example, defeated Henry Cabot Lodge in the 1952 senatorial contest.

[13] V. O. Key, Jr., *American State Politics* (New York: Knopf, 1956), p. 157.

Moreover, Dever received a greater share of the Boston vote than either Al Smith in 1928 or Franklin D. Roosevelt in 1932.

Nor can Dever's defeat be attributed to the conversion of former Democrats to Republicanism as a result of their social and geographical movement from the industrial cities to the metropolitan suburbs. Although Eisenhower's personality attracted voters, the Democratic Party did not suffer from a loss of membership, as was illustrated by the party's ability to capture half of the Congressional delegation in 1954, and to regain the State House in the Eisenhower years of 1956 and 1958.[14]

More pertinent to Dever's defeat were some of his political liabilities. He made a poor appearance at the national party convention, perspiring profusely while delivering a rambling speech before a nationwide television audience. He also had enemies within the party, where local leaders traditionally resist a strong governor who knows how to use power and patronage. Dever had vetoed a preprimary convention bill during his previous administration after it had been passed by a combination of Republican and dissident Democrat (primarily Italo-American) votes, and, to the politically ambitious Italo-Americans, this symbolized the no-entrance policy of the all-green ticket established by the party's Irish core. Ironically, Dever's performance in the Italian wards did not fall off greatly from his 1950 victory. Indeed, he lost more ground in the working-class Irish Ward 6 in Boston (minus 6 per cent) than in the nearby and economically comparable Ward 3 with its large Italo-American population (minus 3 per cent).

Tax increases were another and more serious electoral liability. In the previous administration, a rather small tax increase had been proposed by the governor and passed by the Great and General Court, and so, four years later, when

[14] See Robert C. Wood, *Suburbia* (Boston: Houghton Mifflin, 1959), pp. 135–148.

the Democratic incumbent Furcolo proposed a sales tax, an alternative revenue-producing and tax-increasing plan, party and legislative leaders were quick to recall the precedent that "had caused a great deal of political unrest and might well have resulted in Dever's defeat in 1952."[15]

Dever's tax increase was small and probably fell most heavily on the upper-income and Republican voters, but it was a short-run factor in the governor's defeat. In addition, Christian Herter, one of the "Young Turks" in the Republican Party's reorganization after the 1932 defeat, waged a vigorous statewide campaign, while his unsuccessful running mate, Henry Lodge, traveled widely outside Massachusetts as director of the Eisenhower campaign.

The long-range causes of Dever's defeat and his 8 per cent decline from his victory in 1950, can be discovered through an examination of the Massachusetts cultural base and the changes within it. Paul Dever was a career and organization-minded Democrat of the type that came to power in the urban cities and states during the New Deal and its aftermath. He represented the urban Democratic core, not the charisma of Curley or of Francis Kelly who ranted to the Irish and the workingman about the injustices of the prevailing power structure. Dever's appeal was not to the dispossessed. The "age of identification" crisis had passed. His strength rested on the immigrant offspring who, as foremen, clerks, and laborers had achieved economic and political power through the trade-union movement and the New Deal.

Moreover, Dever had learned the uses of patronage and power while secretary to Senator David Walsh, and during his climb through the ranks of party service. In 1940, he almost defeated the unbeatable Leverett Saltonstall in the gubernatorial race. More help from the national Democrats

[15] John P. Mallan and George Blackwood, "The Tax That Beat a Governor: The Ordeal of Massachusetts," in *The Uses of Power,* edited by Alan F. Westin (New York: Harcourt, Brace and World, 1962), p. 295.

that year might have defeated Saltonstall, and might also have affected Saltonstall's only other close election, that of 1954, when he barely defeated Foster Furcolo for the United States Senate seat.

In 1948, and again in 1950, Dever won resounding gubernatorial victories that secured the highest percentage of the vote awarded to a Democratic gubernatorial candidate since the Civil War. He also carried with him to victory an all-Democratic slate of constitutional officers — those holding statewide elective positions — and a Democratic House.

After his election, Dever's legislative program included accomplishments in the fields of education, industrial relations, public health, and insurance regulation. The strongest and most progressive public policy produced by the Democratic Party since the Walsh-Ely coalition was built on the foundations of politically awarded judgeships, contracts based on favoritism, and financial contributions from patronage-oriented individuals. This pattern recalls Daniel Bell's observation "that the urban machines, largely Democratic, have financed their heavy campaign costs in this fashion rather than having to turn to the 'moneyed interests' (which) explains in some part why these machines were able to support the New and Fair Deals without suffering the pressures they might have been subjected to had their source of money supply been the business group."[16]

There is no evidence to indicate a decline in urban industrial support of Dever twenty years after Ely's trail-blazing victory. On the contrary, Dever carried the city of Boston by a three-to-one margin, receiving 75 per cent of the gubernatorial vote, a better showing than the Boston performances of Al Smith in 1928, Joseph Ely in 1930, or Franklin D. Roosevelt in 1932. Moreover, between 1930 and 1952, urban areas registered a 5.6 per cent increase in Democratic gubernatorial voting. By comparison, Democratic gubernatorial

[16] Daniel Bell, "Crime as an American Way of Life," *The End of Ideology* (Glencoe, Ill.: The Free Press, 1959), p. 146.

support declined 5.4 per cent in old-stock, patrician areas, 6.8 per cent in the small towns, and 9.7 per cent in the residential suburbs. Thus Dever had not lost the urban core of Democratic support. However, while a comparison of Dever's performances in 1950 and 1952 shows that his vote declined by only 3 per cent in industrial, urban areas, it also indicates a 6 per cent decline throughout the state and a 9 per cent decline in the growing managerial suburbs. The new centers of population swung most heavily to Herter.

Dever was not rejected by his political base, but this urban electoral foundation had decreased in importance. Boston, for instance, now contributed 6 per cent less of the total Democratic vote than it had in the early thirties, and the contribution of the ten largest industrial cities was reduced by 2 per cent. On the other hand, the nonindustrial cities and towns in the Springfield and Boston metropolitan areas had increased their total vote by 28 per cent since Dever's first gubernatorial defeat at the hands of Leverett Saltonstall twelve years earlier. After taking into account the tendency of Republicans, concentrated in the yeomen and patrician enclaves, to vote heavily only in presidential elections, the growth in suburban participation must be attributed to the decline in the 1952 Democratic gubernatorial vote. Dever, in fact, lost 12 per cent of the swing vote from 1940 to 1952 among the nonindustrial suburbs where participation rates had increased considerably (more than 28 per cent over the twelve-year period), while he suffered only a 7 per cent decline in those nonindustrial suburbs where the increase in participation was not considerable (less than 28 per cent).

The success of the urban-core Democrats like Paul Dever, riding the crest of the New Deal, the Fair Deal, and the postwar inflationary cycle, was responsible for their partial eclipse from the centers of party power. The movement to suburbia, a declining partisan identification in state elections (especially among children of city Democrats now residing in the inner-suburban ring), a reduction in the necessity for the basic economic benefits secured by the urban party machines, and the general decline of the cities as cultural, economic, and technological centers all contributed to the significance of the 1952 gubernatorial vote.

The Dever Democrats, in common with the British Labour Party a few years later, had implemented social welfare policies which spurred mobility, inflationary consumption, and new social status, and altered the content of party identification for the younger generation. Dever's loss in popularity was thus greatest in the inner suburban belt of Boston where new-stock Democrats had replaced old-stock Republicans. They, in turn, had migrated to the outer perimeter of the Boston metropolitan area making Republican strongholds even more solidly Republican.[17] The 1952 election was a crisis of participation in which the new and growing middle classes turned their backs on the party of their fathers. For example, Dever's Boston vote declined by 10 per cent from its 1950 level in the upper-middle-income Irish Ward 20, while it fell by only 3 per cent in the lower-middle-income Jewish Ward 14. This finding is important because it indicates that ethnic factors, such as the affinity of Massachusetts Jews for Herter and the internationalism and cultural liberalism that he represented,[18] were less important than the quest of a growing segment of Democrats for a party that met their new social needs, such as education, a public service staffed by trained, professional personnel, rational property taxes, and better public health.

In 1956, the Democrats regained the governorship with Foster Furcolo. Although Furcolo's Italo-American ancestry had voting-bloc appeal, the primary significance of his candidacy in 1956 and 1958 lay in the fact that he was the first governor from the managerial and white-collar strata of the new-stock suburbs. He came from a wealthy suburb in the

[17] Wood, *op. cit.,* pp. 135–148.

[18] Lawrence H. Fuchs, *The Political Behavior of American Jews* (Glencoe, Ill.: The Free Press, 1956), pp. 143–147.

Springfield metropolitan area; he had attended Yale University; he had served in the cosmopolitan setting of national politics as a member of the House of Representatives; he had won the plaudits of the cultural and economic liberals, including the Americans for Democratic Action.

Furcolo did owe part of his political ascent to party regulars such as Paul Dever — who was instrumental in advancing his gubernatorial ambitions. He held the position of state treasurer in 1952, the year of Dever's defeat, and his inclusion was intended to soothe Italian Democrats chafing at an all-Irish ticket.

Furcolo entered the governorship with a strong policy orientation, and disdained the petty strivings for patronage and personal favor that surrounded him. Nor did he work closely with many of his party's leaders. Mallan and Blackwood wrote of him:

> His background separated him from many of the Democratic legislators; he was urbane and well educated, with a broad interest in national and international issues, while many of them were self-made men — small businessmen or insurance salesmen — whose education had ended with high school or perhaps with night law school. But more essential was the fundamental interest Furcolo had in broad and sweeping programs, combined with a determined if not stubborn willingness to push for an idea he believed in against the political judgment of his own advisors.[19]

The Democratic Party would not comprehend for another decade the social trends underlying their defeat in the critical gubernatorial election of 1952. In 1960, they nominated Joseph Ward, who represented the party's old urban-industrial core, rather than its expanding suburban base, and lost the governorship.

Paul Dever once said that John F. Kennedy was the first "Irish Brahmin." In the party realignment of 1952, Kennedy was elected to the United States Senate, while Dever, the

[19] Mallan and Blackwood, *op. cit.,* p. 289.

party regular of the urban lower-middle classes, met defeat. This election of 1952 was perhaps the real "last hurrah" for the urban, industrial centers as the unquestioned molders of the Democratic Party, its programs, and candidates.

The Hegemony of Suburbia: 1962

By 1962, vast changes had altered the political landscape in which Endicott Peabody was to fight for his party's gubernatorial nomination and for the opportunity to become the first Democratic Yankee Protestant to occupy the governor's suite since Joseph Ely three decades earlier. In Massachusetts, as in most of the postwar United States, there had been a decline in the populous industrial cities that had yielded the electoral resources of the thirties. Since 1950, seventeen of the thirty-five cities in the Commonwealth had even been reduced in population. Moreover, population losses were greatest in the cities with the lowest educational attainments, the centers of mass industry and textile production.

TABLE 2.4
CONTRIBUTION OF SEVENTEEN LARGEST CITIES TO DEMOCRATIC GUBERNATORIAL VOTE
(Percentages)

	1950 (Dever)	*1960 (Ward)*	*1962 (Peabody)*
Seventeen Major Cities	64.4	56.0	46.4
Rest of State	35.6	44.0	53.6

This altered demographic pattern, explored in Table 2.4, left its mark on electoral behavior. The proportion of the Democratic primary vote from Boston and the adjacent commercial areas (Cambridge, Medford, Somerville, and the rest of Suffolk County) declined from 17 per cent in 1940 to 12 per cent in 1962. In two decades, Boston and its vicinity's share of the total election vote had dropped from 18 to 11 per cent. Consequently, Endicott Peabody could win the gubernatorial contest with only a 14,000-vote plurality in Boston, while Paul Dever had lost two gubernatorial contests, in 1940 and 1952, with a Boston voting cushion of five to ten times that of Peabody's plurality.

The twenty-six industrial centers that had yielded 47 per cent of the gubernatorial vote in 1940 now provided only 40 per cent of the vote for Peabody and his opponent, the incumbent Governor Volpe. Towns outside the metropolitan areas that had supplied 39 per cent of the gubernatorial ballots in 1940 now cast only 32 per cent. The balance of power in the Democratic Party had passed to the metropolitan fringe: over two decades these areas, in which the patrician and managerial cultures were rooted, had doubled their share of the total vote. The meaningful political units were now the metropolitan areas rather than the cities and towns.

In 1962, the swing to Governor Peabody expressed primarily an upper-middle-income judgment on the function of government that had gathered momentum since the Ely victory of 1930. In 1920, the highest voting turnout was among the small-town yeomanry, who identified with the Protestant Republicanism of postwar America. In 1962, the highest turnout was among the managerial class in the metropolitan suburbs and nonindustrial cities, and the lowest turnout was among the small-town yeomanry. The yeomen are the ones now alien to the prevailing symbols, in this case the emerging managerial-administrative political style of the postindustrial United States.[20]

Peabody lost votes among the sensitive Italian Democrats who voted in large numbers for the Republican, John Volpe. Note in Table 2.5 that there was a positive correlation between socioeconomic status and Peabody's gain over his

[20] Similarities in American agrarian political behavior are explored in Angus Campbell, Phillip E. Converse, Warren E. Miller, and Donald E. Stokes, *The American Voter* (New York: Wiley, 1960), Chapter 15.

TABLE 2.5

SWING VOTE TO PEABODY IN 1962 FROM WARD'S VOTE IN 1960: BY ETHNICITY AND SOCIOECONOMIC STATUS*
(*Figures given as percentage differences*)

	Socioeconomic Status		
Ethnic Group	*High*	*Moderate*	*Low*
Yankee	+14	+6	+2
Jewish	+12	+9	+6
Irish	+ 5	+2	−1
Italian	+ 3	0	−3

* Omitting the Italian group, partial correlations indicate that 51 per cent of the total variation is a function of socioeconomic status, and 49 per cent a function of ethnicity.

party's 1960 gubernatorial aspirant, Joseph Ward. At each socioeconomic level, Yankees and Jews were the most receptive, Irish-American electors moderately receptive, and Italo-American voters the least receptive to Peabody. Suburban-managerial norms, strengthened by high economic status *and* Yankee-Jewish cultural values, had caused a substantial voting shift. This shift was sufficient to defeat John Volpe, an honest businessman who enjoyed the advantage of the incumbent, and "had honestly, if ineptly tried to do something about political corruption."[21]

The source of Peabody's attraction over the preceding Democratic candidate, Joseph Ward, can also be shown by a comparison of Boston, urban-industrial, small-town, and metropolitan-fringe votes between the elections of 1960 and 1962. Peabody exceeded Ward by about 3 per cent in the statewide vote, enough to give him a slender victory over Governor Volpe. However, his most impressive gain was a 10 per cent increase in the large towns and suburbs in the Springfield and Boston metropolitan areas. In the old-stock

[21] Less than one-fifth of the respondents in the *Boston College-Simmons College Political Survey,* October 1962, expressed strong dissatisfactions with Governor Volpe.

small towns, his advantage over Ward was only 2 per cent. He ran only 1 per cent ahead of Ward in Boston (2 per cent in all of Suffolk County), and 19 per cent behind Ward in the six industrial cities where Ward had regional and home county (Worcester) strength. However, Peabody did run 6 per cent ahead of Ward in the remaining twenty-four industrial cities. In all the urban cores, Peabody received only 3 per cent more of the total vote than Ward, well below the vote for the new governor in the patrician-managerial enclaves.

This was not a short-term reaction on the part of dissident Democrats who had bolted the party and its gubernatorial choice in 1960. It was, rather, part of a long-term trend for the postimmigrant, posturban politics of the Democratic Party to support policies and candidates that were in harmony with the ethos of the metropolitan fringe.

Although Peabody was to be defeated by his own lieutenant governor in the 1964 primary, the critical import of the 1962 election was that it altered governmental structures and processes within the Commonwealth. In 1960, the suburban Democrats and Independents had turned away from the party because of the corruption issue. However, in 1962 it was not a case of the same song with different words. The Republican "rascals" were not turned out. Instead, the Republican governor was viewed as a sincere, honest individual trying to do a businesslike job as chief executive.

In 1962, the suburban middle class achieved through Peabody the political access and leadership that Dever as a party regular, who had been trained to depend on the urban core for his political support, could not supply in 1952. It is instructive to recall that in 1952 the managerial class wanted access to the political system so that it could use it not as a tool to achieve vertical social mobility (its urban-immigrant function), but as a device to handle problems that bore especially hard on the suburbs. These problems, including metropolitan planning, taxes, transportation, and education, guided voting choices in the metropolitan fringe. The added support for Christian Herter in the suburbs, however, registered dissatisfaction with the urban-centered Democratic Party's inability to cope with these tasks.

Conclusion: Inheritance and Transformation

This chapter, in discussing four critical elections that span almost half a century, has emphasized the shifting nature of political choice by the major elements in the Massachusetts polity. This should not obscure the high degree of tenacity in electoral behavior. In all of these elections, and in most other gubernatorial contests in the Bay State, the Republican vote increases as one moves from city to town, from wards where the social life revolves around the Sons of Italy or the Polish-American Club to those where it thrives at the country club and the League of Women Voters, from neighborhoods where the skyline is dominated by Our Lady or St. Anthony to those where it is dominated by the First Congregational Church. In all of these contests, the four cultural strata occupy the same relative positions on a continuum extending from the most Democratic to the least Democratic. Thus, between 1920 and 1962, the mean Democratic vote in gubernatorial elections was 71.2 per cent for the workers, 45.7 per cent for the managers, 37.9 per cent for the patricians, and 29.5 per cent for the yeomen. The general trend of the state's major social divisions has been toward a stronger Democratic Party and a more competitive two-party system, but there have been significant variations in political growth. The Democratic increase in each election over the four-decade period has been least perceptible among the patricians and the yeomen. There has also been an increase in the electoral differences among the four cultures during each of the four gubernatorial contests.

There has been an absolute decline in regional, class, ethnic, and religious differences since 1920 or 1928, but there is no evidence that the four cultures are in greater political accord in their voting preferences. It can also be seen in Table 2.6 that the period of Democratic expansion varies

TABLE 2.6

CHANGE IN DEMOCRATIC PERCENTAGE OF GUBERNATORIAL VOTE, 1920–1962: BY CULTURAL BASE

	Percentage Change		
Cultural Base	*1920–1962*	*1930–1962*	*1952–1962*
Workers	+22.1	0.0	+5.6
Managers	+18.3	0.0	+9.7
Patricians	+15.1	−1.6	+7.0
Yeomen	+10.7	−3.8	+3.0

for each of them. In the postwar decade, it is the managerial stratum that has shown the greatest increase in Democratic tendencies, just as it was the urban workers who manifested the greatest Democratic movement earlier in this century. The old party foundations endure, but they have been modified by altered social and political perspectives, perspectives that have somewhat increased the middle-class base of Democratic strength and at the same time have increased the working-class (worker-yeomen) alignment with the Republican Party.

A summary of voting and party trends is more clearly outlined in Table 2.7. In every election, with the possible exception of that of 1952, the stratum that has hoped to replace the existing political norms with alternative sets of political perspectives has manifested the highest turnout. The election of 1920 was a return to the *status quo ante bellum* for the old-stock, small-town stratum which maintained the heritage of insular, Protestant, rural nineteenth-century America, a heritage that had been upset temporarily by the rumblings of foreign wars.

In 1930, the immigrant masses, now schooled in the politics of the urban centers that they governed, transferred the

TABLE 2.7
POLITICAL BEHAVIOR IN FOUR GUBERNATORIAL ELECTIONS

Election	*Electoral Crisis*	*Group Showing Highest Turnout*	*Major Shifters**
1920	Identification	Yeomen	Workers
1930	Integration (vertical access)	Workers	Workers
1952	Reintegration, participation (horizontal access)	Patricians	Managers
1962	Governmental process, structure	Managers	Managers

* Group showing greatest swing in voting from the previous critical election.

ethos of city politics to the national stage, and the party gained cohesion through Al Smith's candidacy for the presidency. In 1962, the managerial stratum, assimilated within the new social patterns of residential and technological change, re-entered the political process with an ethos that was unrecognizable to its fathers. The latter had voted for a son of Tammany rather than someone of a colonial lineage from Harvard.

Status, rather than class or party affiliation, links the most politically volatile strata in each election, as Table 2.7 indicates. The two lower-status groups, the workers and the yeomen, provided the fuel of political discontent in the two critical prewar elections. The two upper-status groups, the patricians and managers, performed the same function in the two critical postwar elections. In all four cases, the most pronounced voting shifts occurred within the stratum that was most deprived by the existing political order and most alien to the major premises of that order. Consequently, the greatest contribution to the critical nature of Massachusetts gubernatorial contests has come from a rising political stratum or a potential counter elite.

The rise and fall of electoral coalitions in four decades also suggest several other conclusions. Any three of the four significant cultural groups were able to block the fourth from winning control of the state government. In 1952, and again in 1960, the Democrats learned that the support of many minorities, rather than the support of one urban minority, is a prerequisite to victory in a two-party system. The close elections of 1930 and 1962 occurred because the four strata tended to divide their votes evenly across the political spectrum.

Although a single group cannot usually capture the highest prize in the electoral system on its own, it can effectively block the legislative policy of a governor and balance the cultural bases on which his political strength rests. Political activity between elections, especially in the legislature and in the Executive Council, places an unusual degree of veto power in the hands of a minority strategically situated in positions of leadership.

The major blockage, in fact, to gubernatorial politics comes from the alliance of those who cannot ally in the electoral arena because of a political heritage that irrevocably places them at opposite ends of the party spectrum. The urban, blue-collar Catholic Democrat and the small businessman from an old-stock Republican small town join together between elections as representatives of descending cultural levels to counter the growing managerial stratum fluctuating between the parties in critical gubernatorial elections.

The weakening of old party lines and of the hegemony of the strata on which they were based is related to a strengthening of legislative alliances formed across traditional party boundaries. As a result, a yeoman-worker alliance between elections shapes a new dichotomy between those who wish to maintain the values of a communal society and those of the patrician-managerial groups who wish to extend the broader norms of a pluralistic society to the governmental system.

Consequently, it is the differences between upper-status

cosmopolitans and lower-status localists, and not the ancient quarrels between Protestant and Catholic, old-stock and immigrant, or business and labor, which most significantly affect the elections out of which public policies are constructed.

PART II

POLITICAL RELATIONSHIPS: *DISTANCE AND DEFERENCE*

CHAPTER THREE

THE CITIZEN AND HIS GOVERNMENT

Their hired men sit on the judge's bench they sit back with their feet on the tables under the dome of the State House they are ignorant of our beliefs they have the dollars the guns the armed forces the powerplants. . . .

John Dos Passos, *The Big Money.*

We proved that American politics — even in as rough a state as Massachusetts — can be far more decent than it is popularly supposed to be; I was constantly amazed at the courtesy and respect I encountered nearly everywhere. Nobody called us Communists: the charge would have been too absurd.

H. Stuart Hughes, "On Being A Candidate."

There are few more crucial indices to a political culture than the degree of polarization among citizens and their elected officials. A system where styles of political responses are hostile, where men are estranged from other men because of social differences, and where dissent is not tolerated, is a system built on weak foundations. It is, thus, important to ask how much political distance separates men of different backgrounds and views in Massachusetts; how much control citizens think they have over functions of state government that affect their daily lives; and whether there is more, or less, separation between citizens and their governors than existed in the period before the Second World War.

The Varieties of Political Response

There are dominant political styles that express the meaning and aspirations of public life at different stages in the development of a political system. In the Bay State, four major political styles are discernible: the progressive, the narcissistic, the Dionysian, and the epicurean.

The strength of the Western political tradition affects the political styles of American state politics. In the written and oral political tradition, progress has been the central theme, and public men revive the ancient symbols of Faust and Prometheus to urge urban renewal, economic growth, political participation, and the need for more Ph.D.'s in physics, aerospace, and engineering. Although men are less hopeful about the quality of state government, the politics of optimism and social betterment occupies a near monopoly in the public dialogue filtering into the Commonwealth.

Before the end of the Second World War, the old middle class represented the mainstream of American thought. Its message was disseminated in newspaper editorials, in the bourgeois assurances of the propertied and old-stock business group, and in the behavior of the academics and other free professionals who carried the flag of progressivism, waging alone the fight for Wilson's dream in the 1920 election, and writing the manifestos for the urban, ethnic-labor coalition of the New Deal. The main obstruction to these goals was the greed of "economic royalists." The boundaries of education and technology were unlimited, however, and the newer Americans shared the "American Dream."[1]

[1] See Paul Goodman, *Growing Up Absurd* (New York: Random House, 1960), p. 138.

Today, although no competing ethos seriously challenges that of progress, there have been important changes in the make-up of the rising minority that hopes to own the future. In public behavior in the Bay State, the theme of progress is advanced by the new upper-middle class of educated, managerial men whose power rests on skills and status rather than on wealth and property. Although academics and lawyers are important, the Massachusetts "progressive class" is becoming increasingly composed of managers of communications, advertising, aerospace, and other bureaucracies. These men hope to wrest political power from local representatives of the rural, small-town, and core-city masses. Resistance to "progress," or the illusion of progress, is set against a political economy in which the yeomen and industrial workers are no longer critical. Local politicians and constituents who lack the educational, technical, and administrative skills resist progress as a defense against proletarianism.

The other three public responses are reactions to the norms of the dominant minorities. The narcissistic style, the politics of welfare and survival, is a major counter theme in the political history of the Bay State. This style has attracted a following from Curley to Charles Ianello. The welfare values actually distributed may vary from the Christmas basket to the state job or appointment, but welfare is a persistent need even in the "affluent" society where old patterns of employment, status, and residence are losing ground.

The Dionysian style fights back at the dominant minorities in counter mass movements. The basic tensions of working-class, urban, ethnic, and Catholic status in a society that formerly extolled the virtues of middle-class, small-town, native Protestant America were discernible in the politics of revenge that flared up after both world wars and during the Depression. Such political movements as anti-Wilsonianism and McCarthyism were the responses of underdog groups in the political culture. Economic and political success is no guarantee that antimanagerial responses, based on economic rather than ethnic or religious grounds, will be silenced.

The epicurean style is that of the individual who concerns himself only with the aspects of politics that directly affect him. When the personal gardens of occupation and family life are tilled, he will avoid mass, emotional politics. There is the making of political stability here in the voluntary associations and the town meetings. There is also, perhaps, the hint of agony that belies the myopic commands simply to vote, to participate, and to weed out public corruption. "The things that are agony may be put bluntly: one of them is the fact that men are facing chance and death without feeling any deep social anger in the process."[2] The vaunted stability of the American political system itself, and the moderating stance of its two-party system may perhaps have something to do with the channeling of epicurean political apathy into crime and corruption.

Although the progressive style is strongly held by minority elites, the narcissistic persists among local politicians and leaders who have learned no new political style since the Depression. Among the mass of citizens, however, the greater stability of epicurean self-involvement has replaced the irrational Dionysian responses. Most men do not manifest the personal and interpersonal public hatred that characterized earlier periods in the Bay State. Instead, they have small, daily quarrels that are restrained from the public sphere of civic loyalties and citizenship.

Class, Ethnicity, Ideology, and Attitudes

Differences in social class, ethnoreligious background, and political beliefs are the three constant factors that have split societies into factions. The reinterpretation of Massachusetts

[2] Irving L. Horowitz, ed., *Power, Politics and People: The Collected Essays of C. Wright Mills* (New York: Ballantine Books, 1963), p. 164.

political history in the first two chapters supported the importance of these factors in earlier periods in the Bay State. The question today, however, is not whether class, ethnicity, and ideology are related to the political behavior of Massachusetts citizens, but whether these factors retain their former political significance and threaten the fundamentals of democracy.

One recent study of regional presidential voting patterns found "little evidence that the more urbanized regions such as New England . . . have high levels of class voting."[3] In fact, these data indicated a slight decrease in New England class voting since the presidential election of 1948. However, Massachusetts gubernatorial elections also pointed to a decline of class polarization in Bay State politics. For instance, highly urbanized areas with a large blue-collar labor force, and less urbanized areas with a small blue-collar population, have varied by about 20 per cent in party vote during the last six gubernatorial elections. This is much less class polarization than in the 1930 gubernatorial election, when 88 per cent of the blue-collar population voted Democratic compared with only 49.4 per cent of the white-collar group.

A second major factor in class polarization is the degree to which citizens have highly developed views, or ideologies, that divide politics into liberal and conservative, or wealthy and less wealthy categories. Table 3.1 shows that there are more "ideologues" in Massachusetts than in a comparable group of high-school educated, politically minded citizens questioned in a nationwide survey. However, the divisiveness among Massachusetts citizens is probably less now than in former decades, for which specific survey evidence is lacking. The more important conclusion to be drawn from Table 3.1 is that only a minority of Massachusetts citizens do, in fact, have ideological perspectives on state politics, and that the concerns of the majority are more likely to be local, sporadic,

[3] Robert A. Alford, *Party and Society* (Chicago: Rand McNally, 1963), p. 238.

TABLE 3.1

LEVEL OF ISSUE CONCEPTUALIZATION AMONG HIGH SCHOOL EDUCATED WITH MODERATE POLITICAL INVOLVEMENT
(*Figures given as percentages*)

Level of Issue Conceptualization	*Massachusetts*	*U.S.*
Ideological	25	9
Group Benefits	26	50
Nature of Times, or No Issue Content	49	41
	100	100
No. of Cases	(102)	(410)

Source: *Boston College-Simmons College Political Survey,* October 1962; Angus Campbell and Others, *The American Voter* (New York: Wiley, 1960), p. 252. See the latter, pp. 222–249, for elaboration of the categories.

and personal. Class polarization is absent as long as the broad policies of the managerial progressives do not impinge on the workers' neighborhood and the state representative district. The working classes of the Bay State must be the most conservative Marxists of them all. There is some class politics, but it does not basically and consistently divide the Commonwealth.

On the death of Sacco and Vanzetti, John Dos Passos spoke for the immigrants and the intellectuals when he affirmed that "we are two nations." He was testifying to the fact that in few other states has the politics of ethnic inclusion and exclusion been a more fundamental factor than it has in the Bay State. The bitter political schisms between Irish and Yankee, Catholic and Protestant, Italo-American and Irish American burn in the recorded history of Massachusetts politics.

Recent evidence points to the enduring tenacity of ethnic affiliations in political behavior. Thus, Fuchs has traced the distinctive character in the voting behavior of Massachusetts

Jews, which he attributes to ethnic cultural values.[4] Recent studies of campaign contributions to the 1962 gubernatorial contest, presented in Table 3.2, also support a high relation-

TABLE 3.2

CONTRIBUTIONS TO 1962 GUBERNATORIAL CAMPAIGNS: BY ETHNICITY
(*Figures given as percentages*)

	Ethnicity of Donor					
	Italian		*Jewish*		*Irish*	
	No. of Donors	*Contribution*	*No. of Donors*	*Contribution*	*No. of Donors*	*Contribution*
Volpe (R)	79	89	37	41	23	15
Peabody (D)	21	11	63	59	77	85
	100	100	100	100	100	100

Source: Report of campaign contributions filed with Secretary of State.

ship between the ethnic affiliation of the donor and that of the recipient of his financial support. Ethnic groups of low socioeconomic status, highly concentrated in residential areas, less acculturated to community-wide norms, and with strong feelings of political deprivation, are especially likely to manifest bloc voting. Therefore, it is not surprising to find that the Italo-American vote, charted in Table 3.3, has fluctuated between gubernatorial candidates depending on their national origins. Of course, this political ethnocentrism must be seen in historical perspective. The Italo-American, traditionally excluded from the paths of mobility that have been followed by the Jews in the retail trades and the professions, by the Yankees in finance and corporate management, and by the Irish in politics and in the Church, find that their rising political expectations are not usually satisfied by either party.

[4] Lawrence H. Fuchs, *The Political Behavior of American Jews* (Glencoe, Ill.: The Free Press, 1956), pp. 83–120.

TABLE 3.3

ITALO-AMERICAN GUBERNATORIAL VOTING, 1958–1962
(*Figures given as percentages*)

		Boston		Worcester County	
Year and Candidate	*State Vote*	*Ward 3, Italo-American, Low Income*	*Ward 2, Irish-American, Low Income*	*Milford, Italo-American, Low-Moderate Income*	*Gardner, Mixed (Irish, French) Low-Moderate Income*
1958 Furcolo (D)	57	84	87	77	68
Gibbons (R)	43	16	13	23	32
1960 Ward (D)	47	47	80	56	64
Volpe (R)	53	53	20	44	36
1962 Peabody (D)	51	37	80	54	58
Volpe (R)	49	63	20	46	42
Mean Fluctuation	7	31	5	15	7

Source: Gerald F. Petruccelli, Jr., "The Italo-American Vote: A Study in Ethnocentric Voting Patterns," unpublished MS, Boston, 1963, p. 9.

To summarize, ethnic variations in gubernatorial elections have remained fairly constant for two generations, and ethnicity remains an important element in all aspects of Massachusetts public life. Yet, these ethnopolitical loyalties are no longer inflamed with the passions of old hatreds. The rights of political citizenship are available to all groups. The ecumenical spirit dispels the residue of public mistrust, and the desire for mobility and respectability eventually turns a minority group's attention from impractical animosities to the tasks of pragmatic politics.

The democratic dialogue is silenced if individuals with politically deviant views are denied access to the public market place. How does the Massachusetts polity fare in its tolerance of diverse political views? Yesterday, there were the two Italian anarchists; today, there are the militarists who find comfort in the ultimate weapon; and tomorrow, for times change, there will be perhaps the orator who advocates a return to laissez-faire capitalism.

New Englanders, in one series of interregional comparisons that was made outside the South, were found to be at least as "liberal" as their eastern and western neighbors on foreign affairs, civil rights, and economic welfare, but more restrictive in the field of civil liberties. An earlier study also indicated less willingness to allow Communists, Socialists, and antireligion spokesmen to present their views in the New England region.[5] A comparison made between a national survey and one made in the Springfield metropolitan area supports the general conclusion that there are less favorable attitudes toward the speech of political deviants in Massachusetts than in other regions outside the South. Sixty-one

[5] Alfred Hero, "Political Attitudes of New England and Other Regions," paper read at the Conference on Political Extremism in New England, Springfield, Mass., March 1963. See also Samuel A. Stouffer, *Communism, Conformity, and Civil Liberties* (Garden City, N.Y.: Doubleday, 1955); Edgar Litt, "The Political Perspectives of Jews in an Urban Community," Ph.D. thesis, Yale University, 1960, pp. 100–102.

per cent of the national sample and 51 per cent of the Massachusetts respondents were tolerant of political deviants when age and education were held constant. However, the national sample was more metropolitan, and controls for place of residence would probably have increased the differences in political toleration between the two groups.

Attitudes are predispositions to political behavior, but they are not responses in the real political world. A more meaningful test of political tolerance is given by the 1962 senatorial campaign of "peace candidate," H. Stuart Hughes.[6] In preelection interviews, 66 per cent of the respondents were neither favorable nor unfavorable toward Hughes, compared with 51 per cent who were noncommittal about George Lodge, and 35 per cent who were noncommittal about Edward Kennedy.

Only 20 per cent of those who did have opinions about Hughes (the interviewing took place before the 1963 Cuban crisis) were favorable toward him. The corresponding figures for Lodge and Kennedy were 54 and 71 per cent. Half of the unfavorable comments about Hughes covered his beliefs: "He is too far out"; "They would let Russia gobble up the world"; and, "impractical — his position on disarmament is impractical and would weaken our defense."

It was a minority of the unfavorable opinions that were more personal and hostile: "He's a nut"; or, "Hughes is a professor up in the clouds." Only *one* respondent, however, thought that he might be a Communist. The climate has indeed changed since the height of the furor over Senator McCarthy in the winter of 1953–1954, when a study of the same, representative middle-class Boston ward revealed that about 90 per cent of the residents were sympathetic to McCarthy and believed that Communism within the United States represented a great threat to the country.[7]

[6] Data in this and the following paragraphs are taken from the *Boston College-Simmons College Political Survey,* October 1962.

[7] John P. Mallan and George Blackwood, "The Tax That Beat a

However, Hughes received only 2 per cent of the senatorial vote, mostly among the educated middle class. There was little support for his candidacy.

> All our wooing of labor proved fruitless; the mill towns produced only a scattering of votes. . . . The Italo-Americans, whom I had repeatedly addressed in their own language, had been glad to listen — but voting for me seemed to be quite a different matter. . . . For the average citizen to vote for a man who stood no chance of election was just too far beyond the sphere of normal ideas.[8]

But neither was the campaign poisoned with the venom of bigots and censors.

> We proved that American politics — even in as rough a state as Massachusetts — can be far more decent than it is popularly supposed to be; I was constantly amazed at the courtesy and respect I encountered nearly everywhere. Nobody called us Communists. . . . We proved that it was possible to speak out on the prickliest of issues — China policy, world government, even birth control — and to be heard with attentive interest by people who had not the remotest intention of voting for me. Very few Catholics supported me; but the rest did not denounce me as an Anti-Christ. If further proof were needed, we unquestionably demonstrated that the spirit of Joseph McCarthy no longer overshadowed this most Catholic state. We exposed the utter impotence of the John Birch society and the radical right. Time and again I was warned that the rightist hecklers were going to break up one of my meetings. The highest total the hecklers ever reached was fourteen, and on the rare occasions when they did appear, they soon collapsed in discouragement.[9]

Nor was the peace candidate confronted by the so-called

Governor: The Ordeal of Massachusetts," in *The Uses of Power,* edited by Alan F. Westin (New York: Harcourt, Brace and World, 1962), p. 308.

[8] H. Stuart Hughes, "On Being a Candidate," *Commentary, 35* (February 1963), 129.

[9] *Ibid.,* p. 130.

authoritarianism that has replaced the romanticism of the thirties as the imprimatur of the working class.

> As I walked down factory assembly lines, the workers had greeted me with friendly curiosity. This at least had occurred in the true working-class, blue-collar departments — among clerical employees things were invariably stickier — thereby giving unexpected confirmation to a romantic notion of the working class that I thought I had long since outgrown. But again, sympathy was not the same thing as a vote. It was rather a recognition from decent people who had a tough job to do that I was temporarily in the same condition. Many of them seemed to have only the foggiest idea of who I was and what I was running for. I recall one worker who heard with utter incredulity the news that I was opposing Kennedy and Lodge for the Senate seat. The dazed expression on his face seemed to say: "And what tall story will you be telling me next?"[10]

Although Hughes attributes his defeat in part to the fact that "the bulk of the population remains unmoved; prosperity and 'the deterrent' have become the twin opiates of contemporary society,"[11] the public visibility of his campaign suggests the strength of toleration. The proponents of civil liberties are few but articulate. If a Negro folksinger is roughed up by the police, or a state teacher is dismissed with an ex post facto hearing, a predictable set of voices will be raised in the academic community, the legal profession, the American Civil Liberties Union, and some civic organizations. These voices will often win out because there is no mass opposition to the positions that they advocate. Although the epicurean style of public indifference is a long way from the active rationalism of Mill and Locke, it is more salutary than the style of the America Firsters or the Silver Shirts. Some measure of private well-being increases tolerance for political strangers who struggle through the incomprehensible thickets of the Bill of Rights and the Rights of Man.

[10] *Ibid.,* p. 129.
[11] *Ibid.,* p. 131.

Power as the Citizen Perceives It

In the "affluent" and consumption-oriented American society, the supermarket is a useful site for a political survey because it is located at the crossroads within the big cities.[12] Twenty-six male employees in one particular supermarket were asked a series of political questions by a part-time employee of the firm. He recorded their responses during the course of normal conversations at lunch and at coffee breaks. The men informally communicated their thoughts about Massachusetts politics, in addition to replying to a set of survey items. Twenty-two of these supermarket men were Irish Catholics, full-time workers, Democrats, and high-school graduates. Their yearly family income ranged from $5,000 to $6,000, slightly below the median for all families in the state. It is men like these who form a part of the workers' culture and the background of the Democratic Party regulars.

There were a few *aliens* in the group (8 per cent), who agreed with the statement that "it makes no difference who wins an election because Massachusetts politics are crooked." The same men did not believe that there was anything they could do to improve the horrible conditions in the state. They were joined by a few others — to form 12 per cent of the men — in subscribing to the flat statement that "most tax money ends up in the pockets of politicians and their friends." This did not merely suggest a tendency to agree, on their part, for the same 12 per cent strongly disagreed with the statement that "although some politicians are dishonest, there are enough honest ones to make my vote worthwhile." In other words, for these severe cases of Toynbee's "internal proletariat," politics was nonexistent. These men were foreigners in their own political land.

The *aliens* were only one step from the *ineffectives*. While

[12] This section is based on an unpublished paper by Edward J. Tumavicus, "Alienation in the Grocery," January 1963. Mr. Tumavicus has kindly permitted me to use his material; I, not he, should be charged with any critical defects in the interpretation of it.

the latter agreed that governmental decisions might yield public benefits, they joined the *aliens* in throwing up their hands when it came to doing anything political. "The patrons may look after us when it suits them," they said, "but we cannot raise our voices in public." The *ineffectives*, who comprised another 8 per cent of the men at the supermarket, felt that most politicians were not honest. They did not believe that their votes really helped to run the government. They agreed that experienced politicians were probably corrupt, and therefore, to them it made sense to vote for new candidates who had not yet been corrupted. This segment at the supermarket exhibited the telltale sign of the political ineffective when it agreed with the lament that "public officials in Massachusetts don't care what people like me think."

Because the *aliens* and the *ineffectives* felt they did not have a political voice, they found it reassuring to locate voices that issued the commands of the political system. The same eight supermarket men, 31 per cent of the sample, agreed with the propositions that anybody with money could ignore the law, that state politics was controlled by a small group of wealthy men, and that it was run by the underworld in Massachusetts. Underneath the coldness of the *aliens* and the *ineffectives* there was sensitivity to an elite, the "they" who ran the system that supposedly ignored these supermarket employees. Thus, the politically divorced and impotent were likely to be *cabalists* who found the civic power they themselves lacked in a discernible few who ran things.[13]

The *average citizens* comprised about 50 per cent of the men in the supermarket. These did not subscribe to the politics of despair; they did not think that their tax money went merely to line the pockets of the politicians, or that voting was useless (even though some politicians were dishonest), or that a clearly delineated few pulled all the strings. The *average citizens* were distinguished from the *aliens*, the

[13] See Robert E. Lane, *Political Ideology* (New York: The Free Press of Glencoe, 1962), pp. 113–130.

ineffectives, and the *cabalists*: they believed that they had some political say.

They were not sovereigns, however. They agreed that politicians cared most about the electorate at election times, and they disagreed with the proposition that the way people voted was the *main* thing that decided how the state was run. Nor did they believe that voting gave them a high degree of control over politics in Massachusetts: their daily lives differed from the civic education programs that they received at their lower-middle-class urban high school. The textbook maxims of their youth said that the people ran things and told their leaders what to do. These men had had adult experiences, such as trying to obtain a meat-cutter's job for a relative, or asking for time off to take a long weekend at the Cape, that had produced varied responses from those in authority. They knew their influence over the store manager and state representative had decided limitations. After all, these were clerks employed by a faceless national chain that could close a branch to pursue the flow of suburban purchasing power without consulting its employees or taking a vote. Indeed, their perspective is shared by sophisticated political scientists who observe that "the election is the critical technique for insuring that government leaders will be *relatively responsive* to non-leaders."[14]

The *average citizens* among the supermarket men knew that they did not set the public policies of the laws under which they lived. Yet to them, the political system was like a quasi-democratic army in which the officers made the major decicions, but in which they (the privates) could dilute or expand the policy directives and even vote for a new slate of officers.

After the survey, a clerk told his fellow worker and my associate:

> Aw come on, you really think that we have much to say

[14] Robert A. Dahl, *A Preface to Democratic Theory* (Chicago: The University of Chicago Press, 1956), pp. 124–125. The italics are mine.

> about the way the laws are made in this state? Hah. It's them. It's the big guys that do that.

But the *same* person went on to add:

> I was talking to a friend of mine the other day about just this thing (voting), and I told him those politicians can try to do whatever they want to do, but we little guys have one very powerful little thing in our favor — a vote. If we have to we can get together and vote any rotten politician out on his heels.

The political system, then, works like the supermarket. The managers make the major policy decisions, but the employees, as workers and customers, can exercise their franchise in the locker room and in the aisles, flanked by the multicolored packages of nutrition and status.

There was one other belief that was shared by 75 per cent of the supermarket men. They believed that politics, like much of life, was a process of acquisition, and that money "talked." Thus, they affirmed that candidates became tools of those who financed their campaigns, and that there was much graft in state politics.

They knew, as members of the supermarket world, that the little bundle of family capitalism at the end of the block had gone out of business because it could not offer its groceries at a price that would entice customers from the shiny chromium-plated chain store. They knew, too, that the shoppers from the tenements bought poorer-grade meats, and, in return, received fewer shopping stamps than the more affluent customers from the old estates. As good Irish Democrats, they knew about money and politics from their own experiences and those of their fathers, and they were proud of the fact that one of their own, John Fitzgerald Kennedy, had acquired two generations of wealth to use as an entrance fee to the presidential nomination and election.

This belief in the acquisitive nature of politics often led to some resentment of peers who had attained political success: "I know———. He never got beyond high school. Got himself elected to the legislature a few years back, and now he is a bank inspector. Why, I know more about banking than he does."

It is ironic, therefore, that the old and new patricians retain a share of high public offices even though they are few in numbers. The reason is that the patricians are regarded as trustees with public motives which are not solely self-seeking. The Progressive historian, Vernon Louis Parrington, would have gasped in disbelief if a common man had told him that the few men of great wealth and standing could be trusted with high public office *because they were few and because they were wealthy*!

As far as one could tell, 25 per cent of the sample were full-fledged citizens completely aware of their political franchise despite the fact that full political citizenship came most easily to those who entered the public arena with social, psychological, and economic affluence.[15]

The Expectant, the Disenchanted, and the Dispossessed

In the inventory of political citizenship the *aliens*, the *ineffectives*, and the *cabalists* are categorized as "dispossessed" voters. None of the "dispossessed" selected political party as their reason for voting for a particular gubernatorial candidate in 1962. Only 10 per cent of those categorized as "disenchanted," or "expectant," voted for Volpe because "Peabody was no good," or voted for Peabody because "Volpe has been such a lousy governor"; but two thirds of the "dispossessed" chose this negative, personalized, antipolitical criterion. While 75 per cent of the "disenchanted" average citizens and the "expectant" minority mentioned Peabody's advocacy of constitutional reform as a reason to support him, none of the "dispossessed" entertained such optimistic thoughts about the future of the political system. Unless they are mobilized,

[15] On correlates of political participation see Robert E. Lane, *Political Life* (Glencoe, Ill.: The Free Press, 1959), especially Part 3.

"the dispossessed" will remain political isolates. The Massachusetts Constitution empowers the General Court to make voting compulsory. Who would rise from the political underground to bear the burdens of citizenship under penalty of law?[16] Nonvoting is concentrated among the poor, the uneducated, and the unskilled, and it is these people who comprise the reservoir of the politically dispossessed — people with the attitudes of the *aliens*, the *ineffectives*, and the *cabalists*.[17]

The "expectant," the 25 per cent in the supermarket who felt most politically enfranchised, had a lively sense of political interest. Indeed, all those who felt fully enfranchised were very interested in politics, while only 50 per cent of the other men were so motivated. Thus, there was an interesting phenomenon at work. The politically enfranchised group, like the politically sophisticated with little education described in other studies, was strongly motivated to attain public status despite the absence of social and economic supports.[18]

In democratic theory, the "dispossessed" are the problem and the "expectant" are the hope; but in the urban core, the average, "disenchanted" citizens constitute the majority. Lane, in a study in Eastport, found that most average citizens thought of Utopia only as the day after tomorrow, a day on which all the people would be pleasant and there would be medical care and fewer personal problems.[19] In the supermarket, the average citizens also lacked long-term political perspectives.

Nevertheless, the most impressive fact both in Eastport and among the supermarket men was the strength of the feel-

[16] I am indebted to Earl Latham for bringing this point to my attention.

[17] Edgar Litt, "Characteristics of Non-Voters in Massachusetts," unpublished MS, 1962, based on election and demographic data.

[18] Angus Campbell, Phillip E. Converse, Warren E. Miller, and Donald E. Stokes, *The American Voter* (New York: Wiley, 1960), pp. 250–256.

[19] Lane, *Political Ideology, op. cit.*, pp. 201–212.

ing that political participation was worthwhile. While the "reformers" and the "expectant" used deductive political reasoning, the average supermarket man reasoned inductively. The highly enfranchised and active few started with premises about the political system and then devoted energy to constitutional and party reform. The "disenchanted," those whose feelings of control were more limited, accepted the political world if their personal, family, and working lives were in satisfactory order.

Alienation and the Voter

Below are nine propositions about Massachusetts politics that have been taken from a study by Murray B. Levin.[20] Levin suggests that this syndrome of beliefs constitutes the political behavior of alienated voters. To test each general statement, the majority opinion among the supermarket men has been taken as a reasonable standard of evidence for their validity.

1. Politicians in general are either corrupt, incompetent, or solely self-interested.

Probably false. Although there are no data on perceptions of competence, 92 per cent of the supermarket men denied that elections were meaningless because of the crookedness of Massachusetts politics. In addition, 80 per cent agreed that most politicians were honest, and 88 per cent affirmed that there were enough honest politicians to make voting worthwhile. Using self-interest in more than a trivial and tautological sense, 73 per cent denied that politicians thought

[20] Murray B. Levin and George Blackwood, *The Compleat Politician: Political Strategy in Massachusetts* (Copyright (c) 1962 by The Bobbs-Merrill Company, Inc., Indianapolis), especially pp. 153–154. His propositions are reprinted here by permission of the publishers. See also Murray B. Levin, *The Alienated Voter: Politics in Boston* (New York: Holt, Rinehart, 1960). I, of course, am responsible for any unintentional distortions of Professor Levin's meaning.

only of themselves, and 66 per cent believed that politicians did care about the voters between elections.

2. The candidates involved in these elections were politicians, and therefore corrupt.

False. The evidence just cited applies here as well. In addition, 81 per cent believed there was no relationship between political corruption and a public official's length of service. Nor would 77 per cent vote for a new candidate on the theory that new men were likely to be honest.

3. The community is controlled by a tightly knit power elite composed of contractors, the rich, bookies, elements of the underworld, and political influentials.

False. If cabals exist, few of these supermarket men were aware of them. In responses to three distinct questions, 69 per cent of the supermarket men indicated that state politics was not controlled by the underworld, by a small group of wealthy men, or by those with enough money to ignore the law. The supermarket men said enough about politicians to indicate that they saw no power elite among their elected officials.

4. The members of this power elite engage in a mutually satisfactory exchange of favors for which the public at large ultimately pays and from which it is excluded.

False. If there is no power elite, it cannot act in this manner. Eight-eight per cent of the men did not think that most of their tax money ended up in the pockets of politicians and their friends; 81 per cent thought that public officials did care about what the supermarket men thought; and 80 per cent believed that they helped to run the government when they went to the polls.

5. Public life in Massachusetts is characterized by widespread evasion of the law as the principle for conducting public business.

True. Although those with a lot of money cannot ignore the law, the supermarket men did believe, by about a three-to-one margin, that there was considerable bribery and graft in public life: in a success-oriented society, politics was an acquisitive process; so was life at the supermarket.

6. The so-called reform candidate cannot govern without working with the old power elite, or he comes to desire the rewards of illicit office-holding (graft), or he cannot remain honest even if he wants to, because contact with politicians or the attainment of power will corrupt him.

False. This electorate failed to see the hidden hand of Mephistopheles. Most politicians were thought to be honest, and politics was seen as a useful public activity. As it has already been noted, this group did not believe it was always necessary to throw the old rascals out and vote for new men because time and power led to political corruption.

7. It makes little or no difference who wins elections, for the reasons given in the sixth proposition.

False. It has already been indicated that a substantial majority rejected the sixth proposition; instead, they believed that voting really did help to run the government, and that politicians not only cared about the voters between elections, but also cared what the electorate thought. Indeed, only 8 per cent of the supermarket men believed that elections were meaningless because Massachusetts politics was crooked.

8. Candidates who spend large sums of money electioneering are beholden to those who contribute to them. The so-called "reform" candidate is tied up with, and indebted to, those who support him.

True. Seventy-five per cent believed that candidates became tools of those who contributed to their campaign, but that, since the electorate itself had some control over the candidates and their supporters, there were limitations on the ability of public officials to repay their financial supporters.

9. The electoral process under these conditions is a mockery of democracy since the voter has *no control* over the political process.

False. Although Massachusetts is not governed by the direct democracy of the town meeting, the electoral process does give the voters some control over the election of public officials who will be somewhat responsive to their wishes. Neither life in the Massachusetts polity, nor life at the branch of the national supermarket chain is entirely black and white. There are hues of gray in the relationships between citizens and politicians, just as there are in the distribution of control between employees and those who manage their work.

To summarize, the "disenchanted" constitute the largest political group. They are flanked by smaller groups: the "expectant" who feel fully enfranchised, and the "dispossessed" who are significantly alienated from the political process. As it is important to study the effects of social mobility on political attitudes, so it is also important to consider the extent to which men shift from one "political class" to another.[21] In the perspective of Massachusetts political history, it is clear that the political distance between citizens and their elected officials has narrowed, and that at the present time class and ethnic differences are less destructive of political stability than they once were, and that the fundamentals of democracy are present in Massachusetts government. The Bay State may not be a political Utopia, but it does permit most citizens to have a meaningful influence on its public officials.

[21] See V. O. Key, Jr., *Public Opinion and American Democracy* (New York: Knopf, 1961), p. 148.

CHAPTER FOUR

THE QUEST FOR CONSENSUS

The old-stock leaders have assumed that they stood or fell on their intelligence, honesty, administrative skill. Never did they ask the forbidden question: Why should men follow me?

Andrew Hacker,
"Liberal Democracy and Social Control."

Deference and Deadlock: The Breakup of State Authority

Power to rule and direct the affairs of state implies that deference is given to those who exercise political power. This authority legitimizes the role of the governors and the public objectives that they seek when they utilize power. A political culture may be highly democratic but lack agreement on the uses of power and the qualifications of the powerful. Or as a study of civic education in Massachusetts suggested, different groups may receive differing instruction in the meaning of politics: in an upper-middle-class community, students are oriented toward a "realistic" and active view of the political process, stressing political conflict, while in a working-class community, students are oriented toward a more "idealistic" and passive view, stressing political harmony.[1]

The politics of culture, that is the public nature of style and belief, among the patricians, yeomen, managers, and workers includes attempts to define the role of state government in a context where most claims to public authority are weak. The patrician class had constructed a state and regional political establishment, one that set the goals of limited governmental intervention within the context of the social status, economic resources, and political power of the Yankee Brahmins. In a stratified society, deference to patrician rule signifies that "the bulk of the community . . . does not think to question that this class will hold the important positions and make the vital decisions."[2] The election of 1920 was probably the high-water mark of Brahmin hegemony, while the elections of 1928–1932 indicated a demise of its public authority.

The process of Americanization did more than merely adjust the immigrants to the contours of a common political melting pot; it used the rhetoric of the liberal democratic tradition to deny explicitly the public pretentions of the Yankee elite. Americanization, in short, brought the end to Brahmin hegemony. For instance, the controversies over the content of public and private school education since the turn of the century were fundamentally political issues concerned with the application of democratic theories to children who did not share in the traditional claims to public participation. The patricians, through the quota system, the heritage of Anglo-American literature and politics, and the perpetuation of political myths favoring the status quo, buttressed their claim to public deference. However, as has

[1] Edgar Litt, "Civic Education, Community Norms, and Political Indoctrination," *American Sociological Review, 28* (March 1963), 69–75.

[2] Andrew Hacker, "Liberal Democracy and Social Control," *American Political Science Review, LI* (December 1957), 1017.

usually been the case, the claims of the patricians fell before the standards of achievement advanced by the new Americans on the basis of the sacred documents of the American tradition. In no small measure, Jefferson, Lincoln, and Wilson legitimized the claims of the Boston Irish, the New York Jews, and the Providence Italo-Americans.

While the New Deal environment favored alternative claims to public authority because it linked ethnic group aspirations to the role of state and national governments, the legitimacy of the political role of the business community was discredited, and with it the vestiges of regional patrician dominance. In Massachusetts the only serious claimant for authority to appear between the great Depression and the conclusion of the Second World War was predicated on the values of the Boston-Irish community. Here, a convergence of ethnic, religious, class, and residential characteristics affected public life.

Claims for public authority are often advanced when a previous ruling stratum has lost its dominance. Indeed, the political solidarity and aggressiveness of the Boston Irish were based on economic subordination to the Yankees, a negative attitude toward the Catholic Church in America, and, most fundamentally, a cultural resentment toward patrician public claims. The children of the ghetto, justified by the American creed, found representatives of their way of life, such as James Michael Curley, to symbolize the new styles of public authority. The Boston-Irish political community needed the presence of a discriminatory patrician class, an enemy against whom social, religious, and ethnic loyalties could merge into political solidarity. Once equal opportunity became a reality, this alternate claim to political authority was incorporated into the American creed. The efficacy of James Michael Curley's political ethos died when James Fitzgerald Kennedy achieved the Presidency.

Another factor partly responsible for the destruction of the Boston-Irish political community was its transition from subordination to incorporation into American institutional life. When the federal government and the private bureaucracies underwrote full employment and equal opportunities, ethnic-based justifications to political behavior became archaic. Why honor the elected state official when the federal government opened the door to jobs and positions? Why esteem the state representative and the ward boss when the national corporation provided more sophisticated and broader avenues to the affluent society? The Massachusetts state government had lost its meaningful role as defender of the poor, the oppressed, and the Catholic faith.

This development is reflected in the cyclical rotation of governmental power between the parties in the decade between 1935 and 1945. Morover, Curley's success in local Boston contests was matched only by his failure in regular statewide contests. By the 1950's, the patricians' sovereignty was dead, and Boston-Irish political deference had withered on the vines of mobility and nationalization. Neither traditional, charismatic, nor ethnic bases of authority were salient any longer.

When the political authority of the governors is acknowledged, there is general agreement on the uses of political power even though controversies may exist about the specific application of public trust. When public authority is diffuse, political cynicism is high, there is no general agreement about the role of government, and norms defining corruption are often contradictory.

I have argued elsewhere that the greater degree of political cynicism in Boston, for instance, than in a suburb of the Boston metropolitan area, or in cities and towns in Oregon, "suggests that a big city political corruption factor, rather than a regional factor is crucial to an explanation of different rates of political cynicism."[3] The fact that cynicism in Boston is directly related both to age and to length of residence in

[3] Edgar Litt, "Political Cynicism and Political Futility," *The Journal of Politics, 2* (February 1963), 318.

the Hub leads one to conclude that political cynicism is "acquired as a *community norm,* a part of the political acculturation process in the city's daily routine. It is transmitted to the newer members of the community as part of the local political folkways — folkways that may be particularly salient in large cities — regardless of the immigrant's self-efficacy."[4] Indeed, this political cynicism suggests an absence of deference to politicians, which is not found in Oregon: even suburban residents with comparable social status are more cynical than their West Coast counterparts.

While the centralization of federal authority has generally caused the weakening of the family, church, and neighborhood political influence, this process has been relatively slow in Massachusetts. However, the power of state government has not kept pace with federal influence, and, ironically, this hegemony of the federal welfare and defense state has contributed to the decline of public authority in the Bay State. However trivial the public claims of labor unions and ethnic minority groups may have been, they have at least provided the impetus to political equalitarinism. These views, erroneously called "liberalism," commanded considerable cohesive public deference in recent decades. Now that union and ethnic descendants have been included in the vast middle strata of American society, however, the utility of state government for group advancement and social change has declined. Massachusetts is no longer a battleground for the conflicting views of economic policy that accompanied the major welfare policies of the New Deal and its aftermath.

This confusion over the state's role, with the accompanying decline of public authority, are related to the state's concern with political corruption. In the decade preceding the Korean War, the old middle-class and patrician strata believed that limited state government had two purposes: first, it prevented the rape of private property by the landless

[4] *Ibid.*, p. 319.

masses, and second, it restrained the imperialism of the federal government, an imperialism that strengthened urban, ethnic politicians. The ethnic, urban, and blue-collar strata welcomed a strong state executive and an expanded role for the state. The legality of the means used by Curley and less flamboyant ethnic politicians such as Hurley and Tobin rested on a broadened definition of property and human rights. This is no longer the case. To be sure, people in the higher tax brackets favor a wider distribution of the burden, and people in the lower brackets want a more steeply graduated tax schedule; but the old economic and ethnic-group bases of state political deference have been silenced.

Since the definition of public conduct as honest or corrupt depends on cultural values, a sharp transition in the political culture is likely to lead to ambiguous norms of proper political conduct.[5] Much of the concern about Massachusetts political conduct manifests an amalgam of diverse political values. Thus, patrician political ethics, predicated on a "laissez-faire" political economy, stressed the separation of private and public individual gain, and the restriction of public activities by officials. The yeoman political culture shared these values, and also emphasized the importance of individual responsibility to local control of government. The ethnic and workers' cultures formulated a collectivist ethic in the sense that group standards often judged the morality of a politician's behavior. Now, however, managerial ethics judges institutional goals and means rather than the conduct of groups and individuals in politics. It is not surprising, in this context, to find major public attention centered on the issue of political corruption in the Bay State. Indeed, corruption and taxes are the two most important issues. Focus on political corruption, rather than on political policies, is a

[5] An excursion through the seamier side of Massachusetts public life is provided by Murray B. Levin and George Blackwood, *The Compleat Politician: Political Strategy in Massachusetts* (Indianapolis: Bobbs-Merrill, 1962), pp. 54–68.

feature of political systems that are in a rapid state of change. This is especially true when the causes of transition are largely outside the state political system and seriously threaten values within the system. A major argument of this book is that the national political economy has altered the power position of many local interests in industrial states such as Massachusetts, and as Robert Merton and others have pointed out, that corruption itself is an attempt to compensate for values that are dysfunctional to the official norms of the system.

When the small-town version of good government helps to provide the dominant public ethic, corrupt political behavior is clear to the entire political society; but when state government is utilized by the underworld and the semirespectable, by small businessmen and entrepreneurs, by ethnic workers and corporate managers without a framework of state policies, there is no operative ethic that clearly labels large segments of politics either as socially legal or illegal. It is paradoxical that the decline of any ruling elite and the technological advances of the national political economy have clouded the definitions of proper state government behavior. It is no wonder that the Massachusetts polity is a curious type of open society in which authoritative policy guidelines are vague, and democracy often signifies the absence of standards of public behavior.

Managerialism: The New Consensus

In the past, public deference was attached to persons who sought public goals. However, the present relationship between the organizational society and the Massachusetts polity suggests the nub of a public authority system related to institutions and their processes. Neither the politicians, the administrators, nor any other group of "new men" can, by themselves, win public respect in state politics. This is true because meaningful public status, as contrasted with public popularity, no longer refers to discreet social groups or to their leadership. Rather, it is the tendency of public authority to be incorporated in institutional processes directed by experts. It is this tendency that highlights the rise of managerial politics in Massachusetts.

This tendency is based on four premises about public life: rationality, efficiency, organization, and progress. State politics, according to the professional and managerial strata, should seek public goals through the patterned and clear utilization of public resources. Laws, institutional arrangements, and party systems should be painstakingly ordered over time. This view contrasts sharply with the sporadic and fluid approach to state politics of other interest groups and of the citizenry.

Efficiency is the second sacred term in the vocabulary of the managerial progressives. The expectation of direct relationships between laws and behavior, political organization and public outcomes assumes the existence of a "one best way" to institutionalize the powers of the governor and the professional bureaucracy. Organizational skills are the stock in trade that constitute the common characteristic of the managerial progressives. They believe that government should be run by manipulating symbols associated with the professions, technology, and private administration. To them, progress represents a belief in the unfolding of an optimistic future, a view that agrees with the professional aspirations of predominantly young, merited, and educated individuals. The Department of Public Works was reorganized, for instance, in 1964. The premise on which this was done was that the agency should be more accountable to a governing board which, in turn, should answer directly to the governor. This political development took place after extensive evidence of departmental corruption had been brought to the public's attention. However, it is significant that there was no public discussion about the allocation of resources to highways and other public projects that constituted the objectives of the department. Administrative organization, rather than alternative public policies, was at stake. Politically this institutionalization of expertise makes it less likely that policies advocated in the name of managerial efficiency will be debated.

The metropolitan politics of urban renewal can be seen as another attempt to infuse authoritative public directives into a diffuse system. Discussion seldom involves the need for urban renewal directed by trained professionals. Rather, it involves efforts by the experts to keep their political premises unquestioned in the name of the general welfare. Here also, as has happened in the redevelopment of Boston's West End, political decisions are covertly made in the name of political authority.

The third premise, the attempt to create a new public authority system based on organization involves a desire for public deference by the managerial class. Older motives of political participation such as economic mobility, lust for power, and increased leisure do not account for the entry of this class into public life either in Massachusetts or in other states. Politics is not often a vehicle of economic mobility for professional people in a market where their skills are in short supply. There is no evidence that political activity is more gratifying to power seekers than economic activity, nor that managerial politicians are more power seeking than are less active citizens. Nor does increasing leisure time explain an involvement in politics: bridge is more social, sex more stimulating, and bird watching more aesthetic.

The distinguishing feature of this authoritative public system, and the role of the managerial class within it, is the use of private skills to achieve public goals. A society built on managerialism and consumption has eliminated many of the old symbols of status distinction such as wealth, income, and life style. Politics, especially politics in urban Massachusetts, is one of the last frontiers of life that has not yet been inundated by these national values. It still pays some heed to the old baronies of public authority based on social, ethnic, and religious foundations. Its decentralized systems of power enhance pragmatism rather than authority. State public service, despite the growth of federal and metropolitan governments, still calls men who do not need its material rewards.

However, proof of status is not the only motive of the new bid for public deference; but it is an important aspect of the political goals sought by the managerial progressives.

Tutelage by Institution

In summary, specific ethnic, class, and ideological political differences are viewed more comprehensively in the context of cultural strata within the Bay State, and changes external to Massachusetts politics have dislocated older power relations built on small-town, urban-labor, and ethnic bases.

The primacy of the managerial political ethic in Massachusetts is also related to the absence of other tutors of the political culture with viable public programs. The national communications system holds most of our political attention, and either educates or miseducates us about political life. The decline of the ethnic and foreign-language press, the community newspaper, and the local political clubs has also meant a reduction in other formative political agencies. Thus, a sketch of three other sources of political evaluation, the labor unions, the Catholic Church with its growing middle class, and the educational institutions, complements our discussion about the decline of older styles of public authority in state government.

The Unions: Bread, Butter, and Automation

The "straw boss" organized the immigrant work gangs, the union provided the solidarity of industrial assertiveness, and the workingman became a first-class citizen. In the Bay

State, the formative experiences of union membership are variable despite the common organizational apparatus that now covers old differences between the AFL and the CIO. For example, in 1944, when many of the present labor leaders were being trained, AFL trade-union leaders were older, came from lower occupational levels, were more likely to come from working-class homes, and were less educated and more Republican than their CIO counterparts.[6] Moreover, under the AFL career pattern a man was more likely to work his way up through a local union hierarchy than to enter leadership positions after training that had been geared to union leadership.

In Massachusetts, the union heritage is more that of conservative craft unionism — the unionism of Hutchinson, Tobin, and Meany — than the liberal industrial unionism of the CIO tradition — the unionism of Carey, Dubinsky, and Reuther. There is no single mass union with a cosmopolitan leadership to shape the views of the union apprentice as there is in Michigan's UAW and New York's ILGWU. The emphasis has been, instead, on bread-and-butter unionism geared to, and indeed indigenous to, the fragmented networks of localized political power in the state.

The less skilled, socially aware, and more parochial locals have repeatedly taken different positions from the executive committee of the Massachusetts AFL-CIO and its skilled, socially conscious, and cosmopolitan affiliates. For instance, in policy disputes over graduated income taxes and the right to give the legislature more taxing powers, a predictable set of locals, those most affected by fluctuations in a postindustrial economy, have opposed the national unions and the State Central Labor Committee.

In the gubernatorial campaign of 1962, Democrat Endicott Peabody received financial and other campaign aid from the

[6] Irving L. Horowitz, ed., *Power, Politics and People: The Collected Essays of C. Wright Mills* (New York: Ballantine Books, 1963), pp. 77–96.

national and state AFL-CIO, the ILGWU, the UAW, and the Amalgamated Clothing Workers of America, while his Republican opponent, Governor Volpe, received considerable support from the Carmen's and Longshoremen's Unions, and an editorial endorsement from the Boston *Record American,* the paper of the least educated wage earners. Aside from the large Italo-American base to the latter unions and to the Hearst newspaper, this schism illustrates the tendency of the most localized and least skilled labor groupings to oppose tendencies to rationalize the political system in terms of the managerial middle-class style. This style is more in keeping with the politically sophisticated and cosmopolitan CIO unions whose leaders are likely to take a broader national position on welfare and noneconomic issues.

The Catholic Church and the New Middle Class

There are two distinct themes in the long history of the Roman Catholic Church in Europe and in the United States: the humanitarianism of the Franco-German tradition, symbolized across the centuries by clerics from St. Thomas to Pope John, and the narrow puritanical strain of the Spanish tradition.

These themes have meaning in the transition from the ghetto of discrimination and hostility (a phenomenon recounted often, but nowhere more poignantly than in Edwin O'Connor's *The Edge of Sadness*) to a place in the middle-class liberal and open society. The internal dialogue between Irish cleric and Irish politician has changed, and the external conversation across socioreligious boundaries has broadened most distinctly at the top of the hierarchy as younger men, the contemporaries of John F. Kennedy's managerial world, have replaced older men, the contemporaries of Al Smith with their traumatic experience of the urban ghetto.

The political reconciliation between the perpetuation of the faith and the secularized society of IBM is not easy.

While a Paul Blanshard sees Jesuit power lurking behind every law, Katherine Loughlin contends that the Church's lay societies have been derelict in their political responsibility to enhance the moral level of public service.[7]

Outside the sphere of faith and morals, the political impetus of the Church is often silenced amidst the need to maintain cohesion between its communal working-class base and its expanding middle class increasingly exposed to managerial and progressive politics. The tensions are often acute since the Catholic Church is also the most salient integrative religious force in the community. Thus, in 1963 and 1964, the Church hierarchy was torn between maintaining its excellent relations with non-Catholics and concern over Sunday business during legislative negotiations on exemptions to an archaic "Lord's Day" law.

A growing sophistication in handling political complexities is also seen in the Catholic middle class. Middle-class groups often show disdain for those marginal members who made their rise possible: the Yiddish-speaking trader in the old ghetto, the Italo-American who entertained the overworld or ruled the underworld, and, of course, the Irish politician in the immigrant cities. The rejection of the political type who originally led the urban masses is evident in the public style of the Catholic bourgeoisie. A campaign manager in a recent senatorial primary sensed the change:

> We are going to have a lot of trouble in certain suburbs. In my social circle — middle-class, Irish-Catholic people like myself — everybody wants to associate themselves with the Kennedys. The Kennedys cannot do anything wrong. They cannot overspend in a campaign. If Ed McCormack had rented fifty cars at the convention, people would have asked cynical questions about the sources of the funds. The Kennedys hire a hundred cars, thousands of people, and a private telephone system, and people are simply awed. There are no questions because they say the Kennedys have money,

[7] Katherine Loughlin, "Boston's Political Morals," *The Commonweal, XL* (March 15, 1945), 545–548.

spend it on worthy charities, and don't need the senator's salary anyway.

When they hear Eddie McCormack speak, they think of South Boston and their parents' home. When they see Ted Kennedy, they think of Palm Beach, Beacon Hill, the Virginia fox-hunting country, and their children's future. And which path do you think they want to travel?

Changing socioeconomic status breeds new responses to candidates with different political styles. It can be seen, in Table 4.1, how a wealthy, Harvard-educated Protestant

TABLE 4.1

INCOME AND VOTE IN PREDOMINANTLY IRISH-CATHOLIC BOSTON WARDS, 1960–1962

		*Democratic Candidates' Percentage of Two-Party Vote**		
		1960	*1962*	
Income Level	*No. of Wards*	*Ward (Governor)*	*Peabody (Governor)*	*Kelly (Attorney General)*
Low	(6)	74	71	74
Middle	(4)	69	69	67
High	(4)	60	63	57

* Kelly's home ward was excluded from the 1962 figures.

(Endicott Peabody) exceeds the performance of the classical, urban Irish-Catholic politicians (also Democrats) in high-status Irish-Catholic Boston wards.

An old-fashioned, Anglo-Saxon-Protestant passion for respectability has political consequences, and so does the method by which respectability is achieved. Socioreligious groups achieve middle-class status in significantly different ways. The Jews attained an important degree of middle-class status in the thirties through the free professions, specifically law and medicine; and contemporary Jewish support of civil liberties and economic welfare measures can be traced to the experiences of the New Deal, to the political vote of Jews in the American "Left," and to their exclusion from the centers of private corporate power.

Since 1940, the Catholic middle class has functioned as part of the enlarged white-collar and managerial level in American society. Therefore, the absence of an orientation toward achievement is not the only factor influencing the political perspectives of the middle-class Catholic community. The time of arrival — the Eisenhower era — is also important. If middle-class Catholics often accept the ethos that happy workers with plenty of leisure are good workers, it is largely because they have attained status in sales and executive positions of large, publicity-minded corporations.

Similarly, the absence of new political leadership in Catholic suburbs is due partly to the incorporation of potential leaders in national business corporations. The mobile junior excutive is not a stable source of political leadership. There are gropings, however, for a new and autonomous political style somewhere between rejection of the uncomfortably close Wards and Kellys and veneration of the distant Kennedys. Moreover, increased activity in civil rights and party reform, the breakdown of academic and social ghettos by educated young Catholics under the guidance of academic and clerical Catholic liberals, and a general intellectual ferment that is reaching from the councils in Rome to the pages of *The Commonweal* and the *Atlantic Monthly* indicate the new directions of American Catholicism.

Change takes time and will. Harvard is no longer regarded as the Kremlin on the Charles, and visiting cardinals take up residence amidst the intellectual Protestant walls of the Harvard Divinity School. Moreover, the old rapprochement between Lake Street and Harvard Yard is channeled into new political, administrative, and intellectual alliances.

However, the void between the old immigrant politics and the new political patterns is not filled in a day by the suburban, Catholic middle class. For instance, a check of the membership lists and biographical data for the League of Women Voters in three Boston metropolitan suburbs in which Catholics comprise at least 30 per cent of the population, indicates that Catholic women account for less than 10 per cent of the membership. By contrast, non-Catholics are over-represented. The absence of social skills and the presence of discrimination do not explain the differences: the educational median of predominantly Catholic areas compares favorably with that of non-Catholic areas, and there are significant numbers of Jewish *and* Yankee-Protestant officers and members in the organization in each community. Here is evidence that the communal norms and the separatism of the Catholic subcommunity still retard participation in managerial progressivism.[8] The Catholic professional class requires autonomous and vigorous leadership to cope with suburban politics.

The Universities and the Uses of Intelligence

Men turn to the academies for more physical scientists, for theories of nuclear strategy, and for public school systems that will outstrip the Russians and the Chinese. In Massachusetts politics, academic men act as candidates, tastemakers, and campaign strategists. Yet, despite its educational prowess, the state is not unduly enriched by fresh ideas and political imagination.

There are local problems: the major academic institutions, Harvard, M.I.T., and Brandeis, are national in orientation, and so give minor research priority to state politics. The University of Massachusetts, which now pursues a liberal arts course, is located in the western part of the state, and

[8] For an excellent discussion of clerical and subcommunal influences on Catholic political attitudes, see Gerhard Lenski, *The Religious Factor* (Garden City, N.Y.: Doubleday, 1961), especially Chapters 4 and 7.

therefore does not relate to the state capital in Boston in the way that the University of Wisconsin relates to Madison, the University of Minnesota to Minneapolis, and the University of Pennsylvania did to Philadelphia during the Clark-Dilworth reform movement. In fact, one searches in vain for a tradition of state-educated public servants who enrich the polity as do the "Minnesota men" — Humphrey, Freeman, and Eugene McCarthy.

Another fundamental problem is conceptual. Our expectations of state government were framed in a specific era by specific men. The era was 1920–1940, and the men tended to advance the values of antiparty, and of an insular but rational, small-town America. They were mainly from the Midwest — academics such as Ogg and Gaus of Wisconsin, Anderson of Minnesota, Merriam of Chicago; the innovators of the National Municipal League; and the moving forces of the Cincinnati experiment. They viewed state government as a dynamic, experimental force, a social laboratory in the federal system; they abhorred political parties and political "bosses" who fought to secure rewards that ran counter to sound, clean, and public-spirited administration; and they were not provincial since they believed that strong state government existed in a strong and socially conscious federal union, with Washington at the focal point.

Many were New Dealers, as one might expect social scientists to be, but they did seek to maintain the purity of state administration and of the political system from the contaminating atmosphere of national and state party politics. They were rationalists and had a high regard for the quality of the citizenry. Their experiences in Wisconsin and Minnesota often sustained their beliefs. For instance, they fostered progressive state governments and widespread citizen participation. In the long run, events have rendered their position obsolete even though they still have a slight influence on state and local decision makers through their disciples in bureaus of municipal research and schools of public administration.

Their concept of state government was based on two things: harmony and domesticity. They abhorred political parties because they produced conflict; and conflict was bad because it undermined the self-evident truths of public interest and state administration. The problems that concerned them were domestic issues such as water rights, intergovernmental relations, highways, and state aid. These issues carried weight at the height of their academic and public careers. In addition, they expressed the values that motivated the middle class of the medium-sized Midwestern city. Indeed, they closely resembled their colleagues teaching American sociology whose professional ideology fixated on the negative consequences of conflict and social organization.[9]

Two concrete political effects of the educational institutions in the Bay State have been the development of "Tory Radicalism" and of civic education in the secondary schools. Politics is in large measure an expression of cultural tastes and values. Many leaders of public reform, from Murray Crane to Endicott Peabody and H. Stuart Hughes, share common social, ideological, and institutional characteristics. It is safe to say that upper-class liberalism, tinged by Anglo-Saxon antecedents and a prep school–Ivy League education, has been one major influence of the Massachusetts academies on the political system. The use of social privileges in the pursuit of public excellence is an essential ingredient of political reform. Thus, Brahmin political participation coexists with a set of cultural values (enlightenment, intellectual elitism) that are to be protected and expanded through public life.

By contrast, the formal course devoted to government and politics in the secondary school often seems naïve and ineffectual. However, it does have social and political consequences. For one thing, it does increase acceptance of the democratic creed and rejection of political chauvinism and

[9] See Horowitz, *op. cit.*, pp. 545–552.

intolerance.[10] But it does not seem to have much effect on students' attitudes toward participation in politics.

The context of civic education does, nevertheless, train social classes in distinct political roles. In a working-class community, for instance, politics is taught as an idealistic and mechanical process without emphasis on political processes and conflicts. Little encouragement is given to the new generation to alter the low political involvement of the community's citizens.

In the lower-middle-class school system of a community that has moderately active political citizens, training in the elements of democratic government is supplemented by an emphasis on the responsibilities of citizenship, but not by an examination of the dynamics and conflicts of public decision making. In fact, students are taught to be good political consumers without inquiring into the rationale of management.

It is only in an affluent and politically active community that students are given insights into the operations of political interest groups and political parties. It is only in such a community that a comprehensive political training is given to those who, judging from their socioeconomic and political environment, will achieve positions where they will influence and make political decisions.

[10] Litt, "Civic Education, Community Norms, and Political Indoctrination," *op. cit.*, pp. 71–73.

PART III

THE NEW PARTY POLITICS

CHAPTER FIVE

PARTY POLITICS: THE OLD ORDER

The political culture predisposes men to react to public affairs within a certain pattern. The governmental structure determines the allocation of power and public values that power can command; and the political party acts as the connecting link between the citizen and the government official.

A political party is many things to many men. It is the source of a livelihood, the vehicle of a political ideology and a public policy, and a useful, if unwieldy, device for securing votes to select the leaders of the political system. At the least, "the party system may play a role of fundamental significance at times of crisis, at moments when novel questions of broad policy arise, and on those occasions when great issues agitate the electorate but leave unclear the nature of the dominant sentiment. At such times, the party system may facilitate a popular determination of the direction of the course of public actions by offering . . . candidates with sufficient difference in policy orientation to make the choice between them something more than illusory."[1]

Moreover, the political system is probably better off if there are two parties both of which are capable of assuming re-

[1] V. O. Key, Jr., *American State Politics* (New York: Knopf, 1956), p. 12.

sponsibility for the direction of state public policies. Indeed, it has been argued that "the ultimate significance of a state's party system lies in the effect it has on the making of public policy."[2] The political party system often counteracts the advantages of private economic power and aids groups which would otherwise be disadvantaged in the private sector. Groups which are adversely affected by transitions in the modern administrative state may also use party mechanisms as a buffer to unruly change. The ability and willingness of the party structure to provide citizens with channels of expression is contingent on the composition of strategic party minorities, and it is to these leadership groups that one should turn in order to understand the political system.

The Strategic Minorities

The party system provides a political channel in which demands are made, influence is exerted, and rewards are dispensed. The most noticeable rewards are control of the party apparatus, nomination of the candidates, and preferential treatment in the distribution of coveted values: contracts, aid to education, graft, better mental health programs, status, and public employment. Nominally, all party members share in the choice of party leaders, candidates, and policies. However, as in every organized system, some share more than others. It is these strategic minorities which are the chief concern here.

The characteristics of these minorities are useful in determining the responsiveness of the party system to the demands of both the politically vocal and the politically inarticulate segments of the citizenry. Thus, the politics of preprimary conventions, primaries, and state committees are strongly indicative of the distribution and responsiveness of party power.

[2] Duane Lockard, *New England State Politics* (Princeton: Princeton University Press, 1959), p. 320.

The Preprimary Convention: Rule by the Organized Minorities

The direct primary has not brought about that direct and decisive citizen participation sought by reformers. In fact, the primary is no place to bind the nebulous factions of local, ethnic, and regional interest. Yet the mark of the progressive era is indelible, and the preprimary convention is a stopgap measure in the Massachusetts political structure. Efforts at party control over nominations do not necessarily meet with success because "the pre-primary convention only provides an arena for endeavors to reconcile competing ambitions within the party leadership."[3] Moreover, the success of these endeavors has varied with the force of ambitions and the relationships of key groups to the centers of political power.

In Bay State politics, preprimary conventions have figured in the maneuverings of the key political minorities. For example, the Walsh-Ely coalition of Brahmin and yeoman Democrats advocated a preprimary law that would prevent other strategically situated minorities and their leadership, such as the Boston Irish with James Michael Curley, from winning primary victories that could not be converted into electoral triumphs. The major support for this coalition came from outstate, and from Yankee Democrats who had few resources in intraparty selections decided by a primary but a more substantial role in the preprimary convention. More than two decades later another marriage of convenience between Republican and Democratic minority groups established the preprimary conclave, despite the objections of Governor Dever and many other urban Irish Democrats. The Republican leadership, although it had a heritage of party discipline, could not clear the way for non-Yankee candidates in the Republican primary. Therefore, in order to construct a slate that took into account the preferences of other ethnic groups with significant leverage in the general

[3] Key, *op. cit.*, p. 123.

election, they sought a forum in which the Yankee political leadership could bypass the normal ethnic prejudices of their Yankee followers. Jewish, Irish, Italian, and other Republican minority groups provided the main support for the change to a preprimary convention. The small-town, Yankee Republicans from western Massachusetts who led the opposition preferred the battlegrounds of the primary because that was where they occupied the major fortresses. Similarly, the Italo-American Democrats, and the other ethnic groups chafing under the long party regime of the Irish, saw the preprimary convention as a better place to push their political ambitions.

However, for the next decade, the preprimary convention was virtually meaningless within the Democratic Party. Popular candidates with Boston and Irish antecedents ignored unfavorable convention mandates and took their case to the primary, often with success. For the party, however, these stratagems were doubly self-defeating. First, they increased internal strife as convention delegates grumbled about their fruitless role. Second, the victor in the primary often found it difficult to appeal to other segments of the party in the general election. Italo-Democrats, for instance, found it hard to vote for a candidate who had perhaps defeated a group member in the primary, especially if the Republican Party offered them an appealing Italian candidate.

In the decade before the reopening of the convention (1942–1952), an average of 3.3 Democratic candidates competed for each office, and the candidate endorsed by the convention was challenged in 50 per cent of the cases. In the decade following the reopening of the convention (1952–1962), an average of 2.5 candidates competed for each office, and the convention endorsees for six statewide offices and for the United States Senate met opposition in 62 per cent of the cases. Thus, the preprimary convention had done little to unify the Democratic Party. A party which cannot curb the number of nominees lacks cohesion.

On the other hand, the Republican Party, with a long heritage of internal discipline, career incentives, and strong leadership, effectively used the convention to answer the internal party demands of its weaker minorities and to increase its general election appeal to non-Yankees. Again the figures tell the story. In 1950, an average of 4.2 candidates per office entered the primary lists, and all seven convention endorsees were contested in the primaries. In 1952 the Republicans held an informal convention — and have held five official conventions since the convention law was passed in 1954. Republican cohesion is shown since an average of only 1.1 candidates per office entered the primaries in the decade 1952–1962, and only 15 per cent of the convention endorsees encountered primary opposition.

The convention has been effective because of the strong, cohesive leadership symbolized by Christian Herter, Henry Cabot Lodge, and Leverett Saltonstall. By contrast, it has been only under the reign of Paul Dever (in 1954) that the Democrats have been able to prevent more than half of the statewide convention endorsees from meeting opposition in the primaries.

Two criteria are used in the selection of convention delegates: place and party gubernatorial vote. About 35 per cent of the delegates are chosen for geographical reasons. One delegate automatically represents each of the 311 town committees and each of the ward committees within the Commonwealth's thirty-nine cities. The effect of this apportionment is to weight heavily the weakest segment of the Democratic Party and the strongest wing of the Republican Party, namely the nominally Republican small towns outside the Boston metropolitan area. Here the Republicans, unlike the Democrats, can count on high primary participation.

Second, each local committee is entitled to an additional delegate for every 1,000 votes contributed to the party's gubernatorial candidate at the most recent state election. This method of allocation accounts for the remaining 65 per cent of the delegates. The criterion of party performance awards delegates to areas of populous and one-party strength. Historically, it has favored the core cities, but time, population mobility, and fluctuations in party preferences have reduced this advantage. If a preprimary convention had been held between 1913 and 1920, Boston and its vicinity (Suffolk County, Cambridge, Medford, Somerville) would have received 33 per cent of the delegate seats awarded on the basis of the party gubernatorial vote. By 1952, the Boston area's share of the bonus delegates had declined to 30 per cent, and a decade later the area received only 22 per cent of the delegate strength awarded on the basis of party performance. This was related to a slight decline in urban Democratic strength and a corresponding sharp increase in the percentage of the gubernatorial vote awarded to Democratic aspirants in the growing metropolitan districts outside Boston.

Between 1928 and 1958 the median Democratic share of the Boston vote was 70 per cent. However, in the last two gubernatorial elections, 1960 and 1962, the percentage dropped to 60 per cent. The decline was reflected, in part, among the stable Irish supporters of the Democratic Party. In the elections of 1960 and 1962, the predominantly Irish precincts of Boston yielded a constant 68 per cent of their vote to a Democrat, while during the preceding three decades, they had given an average of 73 per cent of the gubernatorial vote to a Democrat.

The combined effects of the delegate selection process can be studied by comparing the way in which the convention and the general election vote is distributed. It can be seen, in Table 5.1, that each party overrepresents the sparsely populated rural counties with scattered small towns, and underrepresents the urban centers. However each party does give a more equitable voice to its partisans in the suburbanized counties which are experiencing the greatest rate of population growth. At the Republican convention there is a tendency to be very solicitous of the internal party demands of

TABLE 5.1

UNDER- AND OVERREPRESENTATION IN THE CONVENTION IN RELATION TO GUBERNATORIAL VOTE*
(*Figures given as percentage differences*)

	Counties†			
Party	*Urban Democratic*	*Suburban Competitive*	*Rural Republican*	*All One-Party Areas*
Democratic	−5.1	−3.4	+8.5	+3.4
Republican	−5.4	+1.7	+3.7	−1.7
Totals	−5.3	−1.0	+6.3	+1.0

† Urban Democratic Counties: Bristol, Hampden, Suffolk, Worcester; Suburban Competitive Counties: Essex, Middlesex, Norfolk; Rural Republican Counties: Barnstable, Berkshire, Dukes, Franklin, Hampshire, Nantucket, Plymouth.

* Median convention representation (1954–1960) as a function of the median share of the total party gubernatorial vote at the preceding election.

the hard-core, small-town yeomanry, a tendency that has been corrected by efforts on the part of the party leadership to appeal to the other groups whose support is needed in the general election. However, the Republican Party's recent troubles in controlling the selection of candidates suggest that yeoman convention strength buttressed in the primary may cause the party more difficulty in the future.

The data assembled in Table 5.1 clearly indicate why big-city candidates with a regional following have not preferred the convention. However, the relative weakness of the urban areas at the convention will probably be reduced by the continued decrease in population and in the potential Democratic votes. In each party, the urban and small-town areas are essentially one-party districts, while the suburban areas provide the closest approximation to the model of two-party competition. The metropolitan areas outside the core cities are slightly overrepresented in the Republican convention because they have now become two-party districts after decades of Republican hegemony.

More immediately, the Republican Party does not give adequate voice to the demands of its core-city voters, as indicated by the disparity between the support they give in elections and their representation in the convention. At the Democratic Party convention, the urban and rural one-party areas are heavily weighted at the expense of the two-party suburbs. Low-income districts which enjoy disproportionate strength in the legislature are also overrepresented at both party conventions. Since urban Republicans are likely to come from high-income, residential suburban areas, alliances between the political leaders of the small-town yeomen and the core-city workers in intraparty deliberations can impede the growing political demands and strength of the upper-income metropolitan suburbs.

The continued decline in big-city Democratic votes may produce a situation where, as in the Great and General Court, politicians from one-party areas can effectively block political candidates and programs offered by the managerial suburbs.

The Primary: The Leaderless and the Led

The most important effect of the primary in the recent past in Massachusetts has been to dissipate the strength of the leaderless, majority Democratic Party in bloody intramural conflicts while the cohesive Republican Party has held its troops in order for the battle of the general election.

Groups which were once strategically placed can no longer dominate the Democratic primary. In three decades, from 1920 to 1952, the Boston and vicinity share of the Democratic primary vote decreased slightly from a mean of 56.0 per cent to one of 52.4 per cent. During the last decade, 1952–1962, the average vote from Boston and its vicinity accounted for only 32.7 per cent of the Democratic ballots cast in the statewide primaries.

The primary electorate cannot really be considered as a smaller replica of the electorate in the general election. Nor can one expect the second circle of party activists involved in the nominating process to resemble the smaller corps of convention delegates. The contribution of urban, suburban, and rural counties to the 1960 gubernatorial primaries is indicated in Table 5.2. According to this evidence, the more

TABLE 5.2
DISTRIBUTION OF PRIMARY VOTE BY PARTY AND AREA, 1960
(*Figures given as percentages*)

Counties	*Primary*			*Vote in Democratic Primary as Percentage of Total Primary Vote*
	Democratic	*Republican*	*Total*	
Urban	52	27	45	84
Suburban	42	59	47	60
Rural	6	14	8	50
Totals	100	100	100	73

general popularity of the Democratic primary stems from the tendency of voters to be more interested in the politics of the majority party.[4] While the urban, Democratic counties cast the greater share of their ballots in the Democratic primary, the rural, Republican counties are the least moved to vote in the primary of a party that is opposed to their traditional affiliations. Similarly, although the urban counties contribute 52 per cent of the total Democratic vote, the same areas yield only 27 per cent of the total Republican primary vote.

This bias is still more apparent when one compares the percentage of the party's vote contributed by each category in the primary with the percentage contributed in the general election. Despite the longings of some Boston-Irish politicians for the good old days, when a robust following in Dorchester or South Boston virtually assured primary success, urban areas still contribute more to the Democratic primary vote

[4] *Ibid.*, pp. 97–104.

than they do to the Democratic election total. On the other hand, in Republican primaries, the urban areas contribute less than they do to the general election vote obtained by the G.O.P.

The effect of this bias in the primaries has been that, since 1932, 70 per cent of the Democratic candidates have come

TABLE 5.3

UNDER- AND OVERREPRESENTATION IN THE CONVENTION IN RELATION TO THE PRIMARY VOTE*

(*Figures given as percentage differences*)

	Counties			
Party	*Urban Democratic*	*Suburban Competitive*	*Rural Republican*	*All One-Party Areas*
Democratic	+5.6	−0.5	−5.1	+0.5
Republican	−8.4	+8.3	+0.1	−7.8
Totals	−2.6	+7.0	−4.4	−7.0

* Median convention representation (1954–1960) as a function of the median share of the total party primary vote at the preceding election.

from Boston and its vicinity, while 69 per cent of Republican candidates have originated in the populous eastern counties outside Boston.

The voters in the primaries tend to come from the centers of traditional strength for both parties — Democrats from the cities and Republicans from the suburbs. By comparison, the preprimary convention overrepresents the weakest segment of the Democratic coalition, the rural small-town Democrats, and the strongest branch of Republicanism in the same rural areas. Democratic intraparty politics over nominations centers on the urban advantages in the primary and on the corresponding disadvantages in the convention. Developing Republican intraparty schisms are affected by the advantages of the yeomen in the convention and of the suburban wing in the primary; the weakness of Republican urban strength is probably perpetuated by the small voice given to it in both nominating mechanisms (Table 5.3).

The State Committees: The Dominant Minorities

When one moves from the primary to the convention delegation and then to the state committee, one moves from larger to smaller groups of the politically influential. Formal party office does not necessarily signify influence. There are party committeemen who are mere figureheads, and party leaders who wield considerable power without holding a party or governmental post. The influential are likely to hold formal positions, nevertheless, and those with formal positions are likely to be highly influential in the legislature or in the political party.

The state committee is unlikely to play an important role in party management, fund raising, nominations, campaigning, and the recruitment of leaders and others if there is no leadership and support from key officeholders. The solidarity of the Republican Party stems from the leadership of men like Leverett Saltonstall, Henry Cabot Lodge, and Governor Christian Herter. The Democratic Party, operating on a more diversified fiscal and social base, has also been most cohesive under strong leadership from men like David Walsh, Edward M. Kennedy, and Governor Paul Dever. Strong party organizations and strong chairmen are often linked to dominant officeholders, for instance Walsh and Donoghue in Massachusetts, Mennen Williams and Neil Staebler in Michigan, and Abraham Ribicoff and John Bailey in Connecticut. The present relationship between Senator Edward Kennedy and Chairman Gerald Doherty may fit this pattern. A cohesive party, however, is more than a succession of candidates and incumbents. The test of a party organization is the degree of integration during the lean years when charismatic candidates and legislative seniority are hard to come by.

Three criteria are useful in assessing the rapport between

the inner circle and the mass electorate in Massachusetts: residence, ethnoreligious affiliation, and degree of competition. An all-Irish state committee does not necessarily ignore the political demands of other ethnic groups in the party, and intraparty competition may be a sign of disorder rather than vitality. Integration between the core and the perimeter of a party system is usually important lest the party should atrophy and ignore shifting public sentiments.

The selection of party officials does not generally create a stir among the electorate. For over three decades, participation in the selection of state committeemen has varied only slightly around a median turnout of 10 per cent of all registered voters. The turnout is positively related to the degree of competition and party strength in the area. However, even in areas of party weakness, there are minority party activists. The relationships of these minorities to each other and to the larger, more passive social and economic groups can be seen in the politics of committeemanship.

Each party overrepresents its dominant ethnic and religious base on its party committee. For example, 75 per cent of the Democratic State Committee members are of Irish-American derivation and 88 per cent are Catholic. On the other hand, 75 per cent of the Republican committeemen are of Anglo-Saxon origin and 76 per cent are Protestant. Table 5.4 indicates the degree to which ethnoreligious groups in the general population are represented on state committees. Specific data on ethnoreligious preferences in state elections over a period of time are difficult to secure, but numerous local surveys indicate that Democrats receive considerably less than three fourths of their electoral support from those with Celtic ancestors, and the Republican Party receives less than three fourths of its support from those with northern European ancestry.

Each party committee has few members from ethnic groups which form the core of the opposing party. Thus, there are few Irish Americans and few Catholics in Republican councils, and few Protestant Anglo-Saxons in Democratic State Committee meetings.

Each party has about the same proportion of other ethnic and religious minorities on its committee as are found in the

TABLE 5.4

ETHNIC AND RELIGIOUS-GROUP REPRESENTATION ON STATE COMMITTEES*
(*Figures given as percentages*)

Ethnic and Religious Group	*Democrats*	*Republicans*	*Totals*	*Percentage of Mass. Population*†
Irish	75	6	41	32
Yankee	6	63	34	20
Italian	5	4	4	9
Jewish	3	5	4	5
Polish	4	1	3	4
French	3	8	5	3
Portuguese	3	0	2	2
Other	3	12	8	25
Catholic	88	19	55	50
Protestant	9	75	42	33
Jewish	3	5	4	5
Other	0	1	1	12

Source: Data based on biographical material in Democratic and Republican state committee files, and in Commonwealth of Massachusetts, *Public Document No. 43: Election Statistics*, 1952, 1956, 1960.

* Figures give median committee representation for three years in which state committees selected in the presidential primaries.

† Based on data in Murray B. Levin and George Blackwood, *The Compleat Politician* (Indianapolis: Bobbs-Merrill, 1962) pp. 29–32.

general population. While there are individual exceptions, such as too many Franco-Americans on the Republican State Committee and too few Italo-Americans on both party committees, sizable, organized minorities receive proportional representation. Each party, however, significantly under-weights the collection of smaller ethnic groups, each contributing less than 2 per cent of the population, and the unchurched — those with no religious affiliation.

Looking at the combined ethnoreligious representation on the committees of both parties, one finds that majority groups (Yankees, Irish, Catholics, and Protestants) are overrepresented, although there is more parity than in the deliberations of either party alone. Organized and significant ethnoreligious minorities (Jews, Franco-Americans, Polish Americans) are properly accounted for in the committee system. However, Italo-Americans receive significantly less acknowledgment in the two party committees. Organized power structures, such as state committees, favor organized groups that occupy leadership positions in the state.

The social characteristics of committeemen are important because they connote the degree of party responsiveness to demands in the general electorate. One of these demands is for ethnic-group recognition, a role often performed by the state committeewomen. Individuals of Italian extraction, for instance, despite recent defections to Republican Italo-American candidates, are an important part of the Democratic coalition, along with the dominant Irish. In addition, the importance of Franco-Americans in the Republican committee structure is explained by the traditional affinity of Franco-Americans with the G.O.P. in New England.[5] Thus, if one treats Irish and Italian Democrats and Yankee-Protestant and Franco-American Republicans as "majority group members," the members of the "minority groups" in each party (such as Jews, Polish Americans, Yankee Democrats, Irish Republicans) are more numerous among the forty state committeewomen of each party than among the forty committeemen also elected from identical state senatorial districts.

Political expectations and cultural predispositions probably come into play here. Since women are less likely to strive for

[5] David B. Walker, *Politics and Ethnocentrism: The Case of the Franco-Americans* (Brunswick, Maine: Bowdoin College Government Research Bureau, 1961).

dominant positions in the party, ethnic recognition becomes distinct from group influence. In some cases, group attitudes which positively reinforce a competent and assertive woman's political role may account for the fact that the percentage of Jewish women on the committees is twice that of Jewish women in the total population (Table 5.5).

TABLE 5.5

ETHNIC REPRESENTATION ON STATE COMMITTEES: BY SEX
(*Figures given as percentages*)

	Democrats		*Republicans*		*Totals*	
	Male	*Female*	*Male*	*Female*	*Male*	*Female*
Major Ethnic Groups in Party*	82	77	90	75	86	76
Minor Ethnic Groups in Party	18	23	10	25	14	24

Source: Democratic and Republican state committee files; Commonwealth of Massachusetts, *Public Document No. 43: Election Statistics*, 1952, 1956, 1960; Murray B. Levin and George Blackwood, *The Compleat Politician* (Indianapolis: Bobbs-Merrill, 1962), pp. 29–32.

* Yankees and Franco-Americans in Republican Party; Irish and Italo-Americans in Democratic Party.

In each party, one committeeman and one committeewoman are chosen from each of the state's forty senatorial districts. There is no district malapportionment, but each party is more likely to choose committee members from strong party areas. Note in Table 5.6 that Democratic committeemen are more likely to come from the cities, while Republican committeemen are more likely to come from towns in the same senatorial district. Thus, each party over-represents its centers of electoral strength *within* districts. Over-all, cities are more heavily represented than towns.

Competition is a hallowed word to students of political parties. But there are ironies here. On the one hand, a party that cannot control its nominations is likely to dissipate its

TABLE 5.6
RESIDENCE OF STATE COMMITTEEMEN: BY PARTY
(*Figures given as percentages*)

Place		*Democrats*	*Republicans*	*Totals*	*Distribution of Total Electorate, 1960*
Cities	(39)	74	54	64	57
Towns	(311)	26	46	36	43

Source: See note to Table 5.5.

strength in intraparty strife, lose elections, and fail to provide the electorate with a meaningful choice. Thus, competition in primaries needs to be restrained.

On the other hand, a party that lacks competition for official party offices is likely to become dormant, to be inattentive to the demands of emerging groups, and to degenerate into a holding company of honorific officeholders rather than to serve as a vital tool of electoral and governmental innovation. Therefore, competition in party committee contests needs to be encouraged. About one third of the committee posts are uncontested. What does the distribution of competitive and "safe" districts suggest about intraparty politics and its effect on the party system?

In primary elections competition is usually directly related to area party strength, but the evidence in Table 5.7 reveals no such relationship between committee competition and a party's share of the gubernatorial vote. Indeed, Democrats have as many contests in Republican rural areas as in the more Democratic urban senatorial districts. In general, there is a slight tendency for competition to be greater in urban areas where political conflict and awareness are highly salient.

Party, sex, and area, in descending order, are significant determinants of committee competition. The most glaring discrepancies in competitiveness are between Democrats and Republicans. Even when the more symbolic committeewomen

TABLE 5.7
PERCENTAGE OF STATE COMMITTEE VACANCIES SOUGHT BY MORE THAN ONE CANDIDATE: BY AREA, SEX, AND PARTY

	*State Committee Membership**					
Party	*Urban*	*Sub-urban*	*Rural*	*Com-mittee-men*	*Com-mittee women*	*Total*
Democrat	78	85	80	85	75	80
Republican	50	25	40	62	20	70
Totals	64	55	60	74	47	61

Source: See note to Table 5.5.
* Median percentage of all committee vacancies sought by more than one candidate, 1952–1960.

are excepted, there is competition for the position of Democratic committeeman in 85 per cent of the cases, while this occurs in only 62 per cent of the cases among Republicans. Indeed, Republican competition declines in most Republican areas, while Democratic competition is stable in all types of senatorial districts.

The lack of Republican competitiveness may be partially due to the traditional hegemony in Republican ranks. In one suburban district the path was cleared for a new Jewish committeewoman by the state Republican leadership. This was done to achieve a political adjustment required by an increase in Jewish residents and a decline in Republican voters. In other cases, the lack of competition reflects the unappealing nature of such competition over Republican committee posts in heavily Democratic areas.

But these explanations are not sufficient. The least competition of all, in fact, occurs in metropolitan fringe areas that are highly important because of their growing vote. In these areas, once safely Republican, there is a high rate of competition for committee posts among Democrats. Thus, in many cases the local Republican organizations have deteriorated, and the absence of internal competition denotes a hardening of the political arteries rather than surgical control exerted by the party's central leadership.

Earlier we noted the utilization of the committeewomen as channels for ethnic claims to public recognition. The lack of competition among party females, noted in Table 5.7, is also related to this symbolic granting of minority claims since the party places major emphasis on internal party rewards, such as ethnic recognition, to improve its declining political position.

Party Competition: To What Avail?

A high degree of interparty competition is one of the basic criteria for an evaluation of the two-party system in the American political system. The existence of two viable corps of politicians, each with a reasonable hope of capturing the centers of public power, means that there is a real alternative to the party in power and increases the probability that both parties will broaden their appeal to secure a heterogeneous following in the electorate. Sectarian bases of support are unlikely, and sectarian public-policy decisions are reduced. In the history of the political system, party competition is most important at critical junctures.

However, political bridesmaids may become disgruntled, with unfortunate consequences for the community. Repeated marginal losses are not enough. A party must taste the fruits of power if it is to evolve some concept of party responsibility and the skill necessary to implement it. Therefore, over time party competition requires two dimensions: the distribution of votes, and the distribution of key elective offices between the two major parties.

Massachusetts ranks high among the states in the closeness of its gubernatorial elections and the parity of its executive and legislative control. Schlesinger, considering the two dimensions of vote and office allocation, labels Massachusetts as a "cyclically competitive" state, that is, one where voting is usually close and the parties rotate control of major offices.[6] Key, considering only the average party vote for the period 1913–1952, finds that among twenty northern states Massachusetts ties for fifth place in the degree of party competition.[7]

Data assembled by Jewell indicate that between 1947 and 1962 Massachusetts was one of seven, among twenty-three northern states, to divide the governorship equally between Republicans and Democrats. He also shows that, over the same period, it ranked eighth in the extent to which it alternated control of the legislature's lower chamber between the parties, and tied for sixth place with seven other states in the extent to which both parties had equal opportunity to organize the Senate. Only Nevada and Delaware exceeded the Bay State in total legislative parity;[8] and over the fifteen-year period, only Nevada had a closer party division in the control of the governorship and the state legislature.

For a decade, in the twenties, Massachusetts was a Republican-dominated state in which the median gubernatorial vote of the hard-pressed Democratic minority was about 40 per cent. In the two decades following Al Smith's candidacy, the Democrats dominated the governorship and the Republicans retained control of the legislature, so that party competition increased. In the last decade, over-all competitiveness has increased still more, as measured by variations in the gubernatorial vote and party control of both the governorship and legislature.

Where the parties compete closely for power, and rotate in office, it is difficult for a winning governor to surround himself with legislative and executive officials of his own party. Indeed, between 1947 and 1962, "there is no state

[6] Joseph A. Schlesinger, "A Two-Dimensional Scheme for Classifying States According to Degree of Inter-Party Competition," *American Political Science Review, XLVIV* (1955), 1124–1160.

[7] Key, *op. cit.*, p. 99.

[8] Malcolm E. Jewell, *The State Legislature* (New York: Random House, 1962), pp. 9–17.

with some alteration in gubernatorial or legislative control that has escaped divided government."[9]

Some of the obstacles to undivided party government are legislative malapportionment, the lack of concurrent terms for the governor and the legislature, and staggered legislative terms, such as those that require only one third of the Senate to face the voters at a given election. However, these obstacles are relatively unimportant in the Massachusetts polity.

A more serious problem in the Bay State is monopoly by default. This occurs when the minority party does not offer legislative candidates in many areas, so that there is no one to contribute to effective party government in critical periods when the "outs" are given a strong mandate by the electorate. Between 1952 and 1962 an average of 33 per cent of the seats in the Massachusetts lower house were uncontested. This figure compares unfavorably with a 6 per cent average for the lower houses of sixteen other northern legislatures which were studied during the same period.[10]

This concept of undivided party government does not suggest that the winning governor should have partisans in control of other governmental machinery after every election, any more than competitiveness means absolute and continuous equity. Rather, as the late Professor Key suggests, "the minimum condition essential for parties to perform their supposed function of meshing the independent organs of government is that electoral procedures and representative systems be so construed that candidates of either party may capture both executive and legislature. That condition is not met in substantial degree in many of the American Commonwealths."[11]

To what extent has the concept of majority-party control been simultaneously implemented in the executive and legislative branches of government by the electorate in Mas-

[9] *Ibid.*, p. 15.
[10] *Ibid.*, p. 36.
[11] Key, *op. cit.*, p. 74.

sachusetts? From 1931 to 1952, Massachusetts, and six other states, had the greatest degree of divided government among thirty-four northern states.[12] Moreover, the governor's party in the Bay State controlled both houses of the Great and General Court for only twelve of the twenty-two years, compared to an average of fourteen years of undivided party government for the other states investigated.

During a more recent time span, 1947–1962, Massachusetts ranked in the lowest quarter among the northern states. For eight of the sixteen years, the governor encountered opposition control of at least one legislative chamber. And for the entire post-Depression period, 1931–1962, Massachusetts has had divided government for eighteen of the thirty-two years, compared with an average of twelve years for thirty-two other northern states.[13]

Since divided party government increases with the intensity of competition between the parties, party divisiveness is less acute in Massachusetts than in other urbanized New England states in which the parties battle on fairly equal terms. Between 1931 and 1963, one party controlled the governorship and both houses of the legislature 47.0 per cent of the time in Massachusetts, 35.7 per cent of the time in Connecticut, and 29.4 per cent of the time in Rhode Island.[14]

The Jacksonian heritage places a high value on the direct election of public officials, including those whose work is primarily ministerial like the secretary of state, the state treasurer, and the auditor. It has been argued that these officials are more properly appointed by a governor charged with the conduct of the administration. Moreover, the election of other executive officials increases the probability that they will be from the other party and therefore less responsive to the governor. This situation has been prevalent in Massachusetts. For example, between 1922 and 1952, the gov-

[12] *Ibid.*, p. 55.
[13] See Jewell, *op. cit.*, pp. 10–15.
[14] Compiled from data in Lockard, *op. cit.*

ernor of Massachusetts had a partisan corps of minor executive officials in only 37.5 per cent of the elections, while the average figure among ten other urban and competitive states was 66.3 per cent.[15]

Massachusetts citizens like independent attorney generals who do not belong to the party in power. Thus, in seven of the fourteen most recent elections, the attorney general has been of a different political persuasion than the governor. In six of these cases, and during the three decades when the Democrats moved from the minority to the normal majority party, a Republican attorney general has served with a Democratic governor. It seems that Democratic governors are chosen to increase public welfare benefits, while Republican attorney generals are selected to enforce moral norms and the propriety of governmental assertiveness. It is also possible that the older Republican and Protestant tradition or political ethos has some staying power in the election of an attorney general.[16]

The parties competed on increasingly even terms for three decades after Al Smith's candidacy; and as Table 5.8 indicates, the governor's ability to carry legislative and executive party majorities has declined since the forties. Indeed, before 1948, Democratic governors could not find a legislature with Democratic majorities, nor could they ever carry party candidates for secretary of state, a position that was a Republican ministerial stronghold. However, since Dever's administration in 1948, the chances have been about even for a Democratic governor to have partisan control of both houses and of the five minor elective offices.

By contrast, no Republican governor, since Robert Bradford, in 1947–1948, has had a plurality in both legislative

[15] Key, *op. cit.*, p. 207; Massachusetts data are taken from Earl Latham and George Goodwin, *Massachusetts Politics* (Medford, Mass.: The Tufts Civic Education Center, 1960), p. 13.

[16] Gerhard Lenski, *The Religious Factor* (Garden City, N.Y.: Doubleday, 1961), pp. 162–165.

chambers and among the minor elective offices. When there is a Republican governor in the State House, overrepresentation of Democratic urban districts in the House of Representatives and Democratic domination of the three ministerial

TABLE 5.8

MEASURES OF COMPETITIVE AND UNDIVIDED GOVERNMENT IN MASSACHUSETTS, OVER THREE DECADES

	1930–1938	*1940–1948*	*1950–1962*
Percentage of Elections in which:			
Minority Party has Control of Governorship	20	40	43
Governor's Party has Control of Most Minor Elective Offices	60	80	57
Governor's Party has Control of Both Houses of Legislature	20	80	43

positions of secretary of state, auditor, and state treasurer are obstacles to party government.

If the roads to party competition and party government often lead in opposite directions, some reconciliation is still possible. In order to assess the degree of competitive party government in Massachusetts, measures of party competition and party control are required. One criterion of party competition is the percentage of elections in which the governorship is won by the minority party subtracted from the mean percentage of the gubernatorial vote for that party. Using this criterion Massachusetts ranks as one of the six most competitive among several states investigated between 1913 and 1952.[17]

[17] See Key, *op. cit.*, p. 99.

A criterion of party control is the percentage of elections in which the governor of the normal minority party gains a majority in both legislative houses. Massachusetts ranks fourth among twenty-one comparable northern states investigated between 1947 and 1962 using this criterion.

By adding the percentage of party competition to the percentage of party control one has an index of competitive, undivided government whereby 100.0 equals perfect party government, and 0.0 denotes the complete absence of party government. Among the twenty-three northern states investigated by Jewell, Massachusetts ranks third in competitive, undivided party government in terms of this criterion.[18] Using the same measure, one finds indices of 40.0 (1930–1938), 60.0 (1940–1948), and 63.0 (1950–1958) for three decades of Massachusetts politics. In short, the Bay State has met the standards of competitive, undivided party government for most of its recent history.

However, it is important to observe that measures of party control in government do not ensure electoral and policy results. For example, although the governor and lieutenant governor do not run on a single ticket, these positions have been held by men of different party affiliations as a result of only 24 per cent of the state elections since 1930. A party slate elected to office may, in fact, be less adept at solving public problems than an executive who is faced by a legislature of a different party. On the other hand, a governor with little legislative experience and a popular program may be very successful in engineering his legislative program through the Great and General Court, a situation that occurred under Endicott Peabody's administration in 1963–1964.

Political parties are not monolithic systems which coin public policies when they occupy public office. In fact, it is more usual to find clusters of activists grouped around indi-

[18] See Jewell, *op. cit.*, p. 11.

vidual candidates for state, county, and local offices. The same situation often applies to policy proposals once the candidates have been elected. Thus, it is difficult to find a cohesive Democratic or Republican party in Massachusetts except during the presidential and gubernatorial contests. What is more, the institutions of party selection, such as the primary and the convention, shape the operative factions within the parties. Parties represent as well as elect, and the composition of the state committees reflects this dual purpose. We have also seen that party competition is strong within the Bay State and that this does not guarantee a choice in public policy between the parties. A major reason for this is that each party is itself split into fundamental subcultures with diverse political values, demands, and constituents. Thus, although there is strong two-party competition, much effort from each party goes into the formation of coalitions which will be strong enough to prevail at the next election.

CHAPTER SIX

PARTY POLITICS: THE NECESSITY FOR COALITIONS

"It's Time for Peabody": The Maverick and the Regulars

Massachusetts Democratic Party politics includes a network of social, economic, religious, and political alliances that unite, however tenuously, the disparate leadership corps of the party. Most leaders are Irish, Catholic, lower-middle-class products of the evening law school or the insurance field, lifelong Democrats from Democratic families, and residents of Boston and the other major urban centers in the Commonwealth. Beyond this, they are party regulars, professionals who place a high symbolic value on the party organization and the life of its political subcommunity.

In this context place a Harvard-educated Episcopalian, the grandson of the founder of Groton School, a nationally oriented Democrat with admiration for Adlai Stevenson and deep opposition to Senator Joseph McCarthy, a convert to the Democratic Party ranks, a maverick who operates outside the traditional feudalism of Massachusetts politics, and there are the makings of political strife.

Endicott "Chub" Peabody had acquired the reputation of a hard-working, fiercely competitive campaigner, and his

All-American football status at Harvard helped to smooth out some of the cultural disparities between himself and the electorate. But he had also been labeled as a loser, and this set him at a distance from the circle of political insiders.

Peabody had been first elected to public office as a governor's councilor for a district that spans Cambridge and some residential sections of Boston. In 1956, he sought the Democratic Party's preprimary convention endorsement for attorney general but lost. In 1958, he again failed to receive the convention endorsement. After this setback, he took his case "to the people" in a primary against Edward McCormack. Peabody lost the primary, and then made a political error by not accepting an invitation to speak on McCormack's behalf. This error plagued Peabody until a dinner late in the 1962 campaign when his "party regularity" was proven to the satisfaction of "Uncle" John W. McCormack, Speaker of the House of Representatives and as close a living embodiment of the Boston-Irish Democrat as one could expect to find.

However, in 1960 Peabody was the most serious primary threat to the gubernatorial ambitions of Joseph Ward, Secretary of State in the Commonwealth. Since the convention had never seriously considered Peabody, it endorsed Ward over Robert Murphy, a capable and honest, if colorless, administrator. Although he entered late, Peabody made a creditable showing in the primary. His performance was due in part to the many Irish and Italian candidates in the field, but was also due in large measure to positive support in the growing metropolitan suburbs.[1]

Peabody corrected one of his earlier mistakes by announcing his candidacy for the governorship in 1962 well before the conclave of the Democratic Party was due to endorse a

[1] For an account of Peabody's 1960 gubernatorial campaign, see Murray B. Levin and George Blackwood, *The Compleat Politician: Political Strategy in Massachusetts* (Indianapolis: Bobbs-Merrill, 1962), pp. 83–103, 281–299.

candidate to run against the incumbent Republican governor, John Volpe. A very special set of circumstances finally gave the convention endorsement to a man who had challenged most of the Democratic factions clustered around Foster Furcolo, Joseph Ward, and Edward McCormack.

The Making of Party Harmony

The last thing on the minds of the Washington press corps who came to the Springfield Auditorium in the comfort of a cool New England summer was the Democratic Party's official candidate for governor. They had come to watch Edward M. Kennedy humiliate state Attorney General Ed McCormack in the first round of the contest for the U.S. Senate seat once held by John F. Kennedy. Edward Kennedy went on to win the primaries decisively since McCormack showed strength only among the academic community, the non-Irish affluent suburbs, and the civil libertarians.[2]

The gubernatorial struggle in Massachusetts was seen by the national and state mass media as a walkout fight after the main event; but to the corps of Peabody supporters who had worked through three losing conventions and two unsuccessful primaries, it was the last opportunity to push their cause.

Several factors operated in Peabody's favor in 1962. First, he and his organization had gained political maturity through the trials of combat. Second, there was no Democratic governor who could dictate an inner-circle choice. Third, the convention was a model of decorum, and observance of the rules was strictly enforced by Massachusetts Senate President John E. Powers. This was no mean advantage to the party maverick pursuing an outside strategy, particularly since it was not normal for intraparty gatherings in Massachusetts to be conducted in this way. In 1960, Powers had both pre-

[2] See Chapter Three.

sided over the Democratic convention in Boston *and* had nominated Governor Furcolo as a U.S. senatorial candidate.[3] In that year, also, the governor's press secretary "recognized" delegates of proven loyalty, while Springfield Mayor Thomas O'Connor's dissenting band found it difficult to obtain microphones in working order.

It is hard to attribute this change in decorum to a newly developed political maturity. One reason why the convention adhered to the rules of procedure "like a brownie troop at the spring picnic," as a Veteran Democrat described it, was that power was at stake. The citizenry had rejected the state Democratic Party in 1960 because it had tampered with the electoral rules of the game. Any further irregularity would have been fatal to a party that was attempting to defeat an incumbent, and moderately well-liked, governor.

Peabody's convention opposition came from Edward McLaughlin, Lieutenant Governor of the Commonwealth, an Irish-Catholic Bostonian with political sagacity and support. The other contestant was Clem Riley, Registrar of Motor Vehicles, who had little political strength.

Three levels of appeal were made by the Peabody forces in an effort to gain delegate support. The most receptive group of delegates was urged to vote for Peabody because he was a "real Democrat" who had worked for Jack Kennedy in the crucial West Virginia presidential primary. It was also made known that Peabody had gained political maturity through previous political combats and that he supported the principles of the Democratic Party. Those delegates, on the other hand, who were least predisposed toward Peabody were told that this was their chance to get rid of him permanently by endorsing him for nomination in a hopeless contest against a popular incumbent governor. The large neutral group was appealed to through a third and dominant

[3] See Murray B. Levin, *The Alienated Voter: Politics in Boston* (New York: Holt, Rinehart, 1960), for an analysis of the Senate president's defeat in the 1959 Boston mayoral election.

argument: Peabody was described as incorruptible, while the Massachusetts Democratic Party was tainted with corruption. Peabody also had all the traits that the public desired in public officials: he was young, dynamic, aggressive, and had a clean-cut professional appearance unlike that of the stereotyped urban politician.

Most significantly, Peabody was the only Democrat who could win. McLaughlin had the backing of many party regulars, but party regulars alone could not recapture the governorship for the Democratic Party. Peabody played Eisenhower to McLaughlin's Robert Taft. The "outsider" was not dearly loved by the backbone of the party: he was not one of them, and he had not experienced the same kind of political life. McLaughlin, if not the object of party veneration, was respected. He was a member of the club which had taken communion in "our party." But McLaughlin, the insider, could not win, and therefore, he had to be passed over by the party. This was the major thesis of Peabody's strategists.

These appeals stressed the relationship of the decision made in the convention to the larger group of Democrats who would participate in the primaries and, beyond them, to the general electorate which would choose a governor in November. The strategy was to link Peabody with forces that were external to the convention. Peabody's supporters packed the galleries and employed sophisticated communication techniques. These included walkie-talkies, sound-trucks which directed messages to the delegates during recesses, a Peabody newspaper, and publicity blurbs which were released to coincide with the time schedules of the Boston and Springfield newspapers.

"It's time for Peabody," was the message conveyed. It was an open-ended message, indicating that it was time for an underdog, a Yankee Democrat, a representative of the metropolitan suburbs. The techniques employed expressed essentially the language of the party regulars and of the professionals; they stated that it was time to regain the main seat of political power in the Commonwealth and that Peabody, as they all knew, was the man to do it for the Democratic Party.

Peabody won the convention's endorsement on the second ballot. Neither Peabody, nor McLaughlin, could obtain a majority on the first ballot because of Registrar Riley's small, but significant, cluster of support. He refused to withdraw and to instruct his small following to vote for either of the major candidates. It is probable that McLaughlin lost more than Peabody through this failure to win a first-ballot victory. The lieutenant governor was the insider, the titular head of the party, and his inability to win early increased the chances for an outsider like Peabody.

There is evidence to support this conclusion. First, although Clem Riley was a party regular who might have influenced some of his supporters to switch to McLaughlin, Peabody, in fact, held second-ballot pledges from Riley's supporters in the Essex County and North Shore delegations. Second, 125 delegates, 7 per cent of the total, did not vote in the second gubernatorial ballot. While 9 per cent of those in the delegations carried by McLaughlin failed to vote, only 6 per cent did not vote in the delegations carried by Peabody. The importance of this net difference of about sixteen votes is indicated by the close outcome of the crucial second ballot (Table 6.1).

The pattern of voting by the delegations (one from each of the forty senatorial districts) is complex. There is no simple East-West, urban-rural, or intraparty schism that marks the dominant cleavage. In the past, gubernatorial voting has tended to be related to primary and general election divisions within the state. In fact, McLaughlin received strong support from areas where Joseph Ward did well in the 1960 gubernatorial primary — the strongly Democratic areas in Ward's home county, Worcester.

A second consideration that helps to interpret the delegate

division between Peabody and the lieutenant governor is the relationship between political leadership and political patronage. Leadership is likely to be strongest in delegations headed by key political officeholders, such as senior state

TABLE 6.1
SECOND-BALLOT VOTE IN GUBERNATORIAL CONTEST, 1962 DEMOCRATIC CONVENTION

	Distribution of Total Vote		*Distribution of Major Candidate Vote*	
Candidates	*No.*	*Percentage*	*No.*	*Percentage*
Peabody	752	44.0	752	51.2
McLaughlin	735	43.0	735	48.8
Riley	102	6.0	—	—
Blanks	125	7.0	—	—
Totals	1714	100.0	1407	100.0

representatives, senators, and mayors. John Shea, the powerful mayor of Worcester, was able to provide McLaughlin with a 31–5 margin in the first Worcester district, while Representative Michael Paul Feeney of Boston was instrumental in drawing twenty-three of the thirty-two votes cast in the sixth Suffolk district over to Peabody.[4] More generally, these urban delegations are strongly Democratic.

In addition, one expects some degree of leadership, capable of providing clues to uncertain delegates, in strong Republican areas where the faithful courthouse gang of the minority carries the party's banners into the strong wind of predominantly Republican local sentiment. Less clear political leadership is likely in transitional and marginal areas which are marked by a high degree of two-party competitiveness.

[4] Peabody's efforts to reciprocate were less successful. In 1963, Feeney failed in his bid to unseat House Speaker Thompson despite the overt support of the new governor.

A further consideration is that the allocation of political rewards is more certain for delegates from one-party areas. Fenton has demonstrated, for Kentucky and other border states, the extent to which Democratic Party leaders from Republican strongholds support "administration candidates" in primary elections.[5] The reason he has found for this is that the party faithfuls in areas controlled locally by the enemy are highly dependent on party patronage from the state capital.

In the divided government that marked the administration of Republican Governor Volpe from 1960 to 1962, McLaughlin, the lieutenant governor was the key figure in channeling Democratic Party claims through the governor's office, the state legislature, and the Executive Council. One would expect that sensitivity to party rewards would be extremely acute among loyalists in senatorial districts where Republicans controlled state and local legislative positions. At the same time, leaders in strongly Democratic areas are less likely to be affected by changes in the governorship. Access to key political officeholders such as the lieutenant governor is important, and is reinforced by the dominant cultural characteristics of the democracy in Massachusetts. In fact one-party areas are most likely to be cohesive in gubernatorial balloting.

The combination of leadership, reward factors, and degree of party competition, also correlates with the convention vote. Table 6.2 reveals that McLaughlin's main support came from one-party areas of the state where identification with the inner party and hopes of political rewards were best served by supporting the incumbent lieutenant governor. The one-party Democratic districts included large numbers of Italo-American delegates who were highly dependent on the intermediate levels of political access provided by the lieutenant governor and by the Executive Council. Their support of

[5] John H. Fenton, *Politics in the Border States* (New Orleans: The Hauser Press, 1957), pp. 14–81.

McLaughlin was strengthened by a desire to prevent him from again occupying his present office so that a fellow Italo-American, Francis Bellotti, could receive the convention's endorsement for this position. Meanwhile, Peabody made

TABLE 6.2

PARTY COMPETITION AND DEMOCRATIC CONVENTION VOTE, 1962

Percentage of Delegations Carried By:	*Safe* Republican Districts*	*Safe* Democratic Districts*	*All Safe Districts*	*Marginal Districts*
Peabody	38	46	40	57
McLaughlin	62	54	60	43
No. of Delegations	(13)	(13)	(26)	(14)

Source: Commonwealth of Massachusetts, *Public Document No. 43: Election Statistics,* 1962; and official delegate count, Democratic Preprimary Convention, Springfield, 1962.

* Safe districts are those carried by either party with at least 55 per cent of vote cast for both houses of legislature, 1960.

his best showing among the least cohesive delegations from transitional, suburban, two-party areas where the delegates strongly identified with him.

The preprimary endorsements of the Massachusetts Democratic Party have seldom carried much weight. It is usual for a candidate to enter the primary only after failing to receive the convention endorsement. This pattern was continued in 1962. Among the Democrats primary contests were held over the candidacies for U.S. senator, attorney general, and lieutenant governor. Contrary to the usual definitiveness of the G.O.P.'s preprimary convention endorsement, the Republicans followed suit with intraparty squabbles over the candidacies for U.S. senator and attorney general. However, only Clem Riley challenged Peabody in the September Democratic primary, and the challenge was easily parried by a margin of four to one.

Peabody's supporters were pleasantly surprised by this

turn of events. They had anticipated a bitter primary battle for several reasons. First of all, since Lieutenant Governor McLaughlin had a strong political following, he might have sought the governorship. In the second place, Peabody had antagonized many of the political factions in the state, and a "Stop Peabody" movement, centered among the supporters of Ward, Furcolo, McCormack, and McLaughlin, was a distinct possibility. In addition, Edward M. Kennedy was the likely head of the party's ticket in November, and the magic of the Kennedy name held attraction to potential coat-tail riders. Finally, since the traditional cultural base of the Democratic Party was cool toward Peabody, it was likely that it would support an attractive alternative candidate.

McLaughlin, however, accepted a lucrative position with the Metropolitan Transit Authority, and support failed to coalesce around any other strong contestant. Many believed that Governor Volpe would be re-elected. This belief influenced judgments about the utility of waging a bitter primary fight against Peabody, the availability of money from party contributors, and the enthusiasm of the party workers. Moreover, the Democratic penchant for squabbling and for questionable political behavior had cost the party the governorship in 1960. It was likely, therefore, to cost the party the governorship again, since a contest against Peabody would lead to ethnic and religious attacks from the less responsible elements in the party. McLaughlin, who was not a "professional" Irish Catholic, was well aware of the degenerative processes that could be set in motion if he conducted a primary campaign against Peabody.

In short, the political costs seemed to exceed the potential rewards that could result from a primary victory over Peabody. Party leaders who thought along the same lines were at least neutral in their attitudes toward Peabody and any other serious primary contestant. Thus, the convention victory gave Peabody the token support of his party through the harmony of self-preservation.

The Problems of the Candidate

Peabody's convention victory effectively neutralized the opposition to his candidacy within his own party. It did not, however, convert the lethargic and fragmented resources of the party to active support on his behalf in the general election campaign; and, without the support of the workers' politicians, there was little hope of winning the votes of the working class in the cities. Any Democratic gubernatorial candidate would have encountered this same problem to some degree, and would have been competing with an incumbent governor who had broad public support, or at least was not disliked, an Italo-American who appealed to an important ethnic bloc. Thus, any candidate would have had to weld a campaign organization from the loose factions of the Massachusetts Democrats.

Peabody's problems as a Massachusetts Democrat, however, differed from those of most others. A Protestant had not been elected governor of the Commonwealth on the Democratic slate since 1932. The Peabody camp was very concerned about the negative effects of ethnic and religious elements in the campaign. Numerous copies of a warning against "voting your own kind" were reprinted from an article by Monsignor Lally in *The Pilot,* the diocesan organ of Cardinal Cushing. Individuals with common Irish-Catholic and Italo-Catholic names were given prominence in the Peabody organization and on its auxiliary committees. Their names, rather than the names of Peabody's Jewish campaign managers, or of the large number of Jews and Protestants in the inner circle, were given wide coverage in the publicity releases to the state, Boston, and neighborhood media.

Beyond these problems, the main handicaps facing Peabody were the nebulous character of Democratic Party identification in the state and the communications in the party channels between a statewide candidate and the urban roots of the party's electoral base.

Within the American party system, loose and varied party identifications are common. However, the party cleavage that faced Peabody was particularly pronounced: there has been a historical cleavage in Massachusetts between issue-oriented partisans identifying with the national party, and localistic, conservative "Al Smith Democrats." Moreover, survey evidence from a representative Democratic ward, presented in Table 6.3, noted the predominance of individuals who were

TABLE 6.3
POLITICAL ATTITUDES AMONG DEMOCRATIC PARTY IDENTIFIERS, 1962
(*Figures given as percentages*)

Support of Economic Welfare Policies	*Support of Civil Liberties*	
	High	*Low*
High	9	81
Low	91	19
No. of Cases	(52)	(140)

Source: *Boston College-Simmons College Political Survey*, October 1962.

"liberal" on economic welfare policies, but "illiberal" on the exercise of civil liberties. In addition, only 20 per cent of the Democrats surveyed identified with the party because of its position on public issues. Traditional group attachments and loyalties accounted for the primary basis of Democratic affiliation in 31 per cent of the cases, while the remaining 49 per cent used neither issue positions nor traditional group loyalties to sustain their party affiliation.[6]

Moreover, many of the party regulars who acted as public-opinion leaders between the candidates and the electorate came from the core cities which were overrepresented in

[6] Data from *Boston College-Simmons College Political Survey*, October 1962.

Democratic legislative and party councils. By contrast, Peabody's organization reflected the managerial ethos of the young, the professional, and the suburbanite. These people had little rapport with the phalanx of ward and precinct workers who mobilized the party vote in Worcester and Fall River, Brockton and Boston. The latter included many "Al Smith traditionalists," and those who made a living off Democratic politics; and they were aloof to the young interloper whose political orientation was alien to their own view of politics. Therefore, it was one thing for the Peabody adherents to assemble an organization of "Citizens For Peabody" in suburban enclaves. It was another to engage the efforts of the party's backbone.

The gap between these two political worlds is revealed by an illustration. In the usual round of campaign appearances, Peabody's articulate and attractive wife played a prominent role. A key member of the Peabody staff reports on the reactions to her efforts:

> When we have dinners of this kind for "Chub," it is interesting to observe the reactions to Toni (Mrs. Peabody) among the women. She is loved by the younger women, especially those, I think, who are Jews and Protestants. But the older women, especially the Irish Catholics, don't warm up to her. They wonder who is running, he or she.

Within the dominant subcultural patterns — in which a woman does not push her husband's career, and public life is basically reserved for men — the Peabody campaign effort was resisted.

The disparities between Peabody and the Democratic political culture would have been less noticeable if there had been extreme dissatisfaction with the incumbent governor. Such feelings could have been exploited effectively in a typical campaign to "throw the rascals out." However, no such evidence of dissatisfaction was discernible a month before the election (Table 6.4).

Indeed, Peabody was not known at all by 50 per cent of the voters questioned during a survey in October. In New Bedford the figure was 63 per cent, and in Fall River 60 per cent of those sampled. Both these cities are Democratic

TABLE 6.4
GOVERNOR VOLPE'S STANDING WITH ELECTORATE, OCTOBER 1962

	Percentage satisfied with Volpe
Boston Globe Surveys:	
Statewide (sample: 388)	67
Holyoke, Ward 5B	63
Northampton, Ward 2A	73
B. C.-Simmons College Survey:	
Boston, Ward 20 (sample: 292)	69

Source: *Boston Globe*, October 8, 1962, pp. 1, 17; *Boston College-Simmons College Political Survey.*

strongholds.[7] The more intensive survey in Boston also revealed the extent to which the Democratic standard-bearer was unknown in areas of Democratic strength. Only 29 per cent of the respondents in West Roxbury (Ward 20) expressed either a favorable or unfavorable opinion on Peabody, while 69 per cent were able to express an opinion on the incumbent Republican governor (Table 6.5).[8]

It is also instructive to note that the lack of awareness about Peabody, who had actually sought statewide office at three party conventions and in two party primaries, was concentrated in those areas where the intermediary links of party leaders and opinion makers were least receptive to his candidacy. Therefore, Peabody was effectively blocked out

[7] *Ibid.*; and the *Boston Globe*, October 8, 1962, pp. 1, 17. In lieu of a statewide survey, Boston's Ward 20 is probably the best single barometer of gubernatorial voting in the state. With slight fluctuation, it has always yielded the Democratic candidate 3 per cent more of the vote than he has received in the entire state.

[8] *Political Survey, op. cit.*

of the political communications network in many core-city Democratic strongholds.

The lack of rapport between Peabody, the regular party workers, and the rank and file of the party was registered

TABLE 6.5

ATTITUDE TOWARD GUBERNATORIAL CANDIDATES IN WEST ROXBURY (WARD 20, BOSTON), OCTOBER 1962

Attitude Toward Candidates		*Percentage*
Favored Peabody:	Against Volpe	10
	Neutral toward Volpe	7
Neutral toward Peabody:	Against Volpe	11
Neutral toward Both Candidates		24
Favored Volpe:	Against Peabody	12
	Neutral toward Peabody	36
		100
Favorable toward:	Volpe	48
	Peabody	17
Neutral toward:	Volpe	31
	Peabody	71
Unfavorable toward:	Volpe	21
	Peabody	12

Source: *Boston College-Simmons College Political Survey.*

in pre-election voting preferences. Soundings in Democratic areas indicated that Peabody would probably lose about a third of the nominal Democrats to Governor Volpe, and that he would trail the unsuccessful Democratic nominee of 1960, Joseph Ward, in areas of normal party strength. Table 6.6 presents the voting preferences in selected areas, and the projected total Peabody share of the vote. Table 6.7 reviews the distribution of gubernatorial preferences by party identification.

Peabody's camp attempted to increase its candidate's exposure around the state through as vigorous a gubernatorial campaign as had ever been conducted between Cape Cod and the Berkshires. A station wagon equipped with a special

TABLE 6.6

SURVEY DATA FOR GUBERNATORIAL ELECTION, OCTOBER 1962
(*Figures given as percentages*)

Boston Globe Surveys

	State	*Holyoke (5B)* *	*Northampton (2A)*
Preference			
Peabody	43	32	41
Volpe	51	40	47
Undecided	6	28	12
Projected Vote:			
Peabody	46	56	47
Ward (1960)	47	59	46
No. of cases†	(328)	(—)	(—)

Boston College-Simmons College Survey

	Boston (Ward 20)	*Boston (Ward 10)*
Preference		
Peabody	35	70
Volpe	43	30
Undecided	22	0
Projected Vote:		
Peabody	48	70
Ward (1960)	50	71
No. of cases	(292)	(22)

Source: *Boston Globe*, October 8, 1962, pp. 1, 17; *Boston College-Simmons College Political Survey.*

* The Holyoke sample had 40 per cent registered Democrats, 48 per cent registered Independents, and 12 per cent registered Republicans.

† The sample size for the Holyoke and Northampton surveys is not known.

platform and public address system served as a twentieth-century white charger for the Democratic nominee. However, in the drowsiness of summer, Peabody's pollsters thought that Governor Volpe was ahead in the city of Boston. Even after Labor Day and the World Series, when the average Democrat turned his attention to the political ring, prognos-

TABLE 6.7
PARTY IDENTIFICATION AND GUBERNATORIAL PREFERENCE, 1962
(*Figures given as percentages*)

*Boston Globe State Survey**

	Democrats	*Independents*	*Republicans*
Preference:			
Peabody	46	26	6
Undecided	21	38	16
Volpe	33	36	78

Ward 20, Boston

	Democrats	*Independents*	*Republicans*
Preference:			
Peabody	45	24	14
Undecided	21	36	12
Volpe	34	40	74

Source: *Boston Globe*, October 8, 1962, pp. 1, 17; *Boston College-Simmons College Political Survey*.

* Party affiliation is measured by registration for the *Globe* survey and by respondent's indentification for the Ward 20 survey.

ticators on both sides doubted if Peabody had a lead of more than 25,000 votes in Democratic Boston, less than half the plurality that was needed to counter Republican sentiments in the smaller towns. Peabody's suburban appeal was useless unless he could recapture his party's declining, but still vital, urban base. Here, other strategies were needed.

The Ranks Receive Their Marching Orders

It is ironic that the political structure of this essentially Catholic state usually resembles a collection of fundamentalist Protestant sects. A major political figure can superimpose his will on this fragmentation — as John F. Kennedy did in his political ascent to the Presidency, and as his youngest brother, Edward Kennedy, did in his campaign for the United States Senate. A figure of lesser political stature, however, can only attempt to assemble a winning coalition with the unreliable paste and glue of the Massachusetts political groupings. It is only if he is fortunate that he can bring a stronger force to bear on the state's political mélange.

Endicott Peabody was fortunate. One Kennedy headed the Democratic ticket in 1962, and a second Kennedy took a decided interest in the gubernatorial campaign. The President had several reasons to allot a small share of his time to the gubernatorial contest in Massachusetts. Peabody had been a strong supporter of Kennedy before the Los Angeles convention; he had also campaigned vigorously for the President in the crucial West Virginia primary. He had the political orientation of the national Democratic party; he also shared the cultural affinities of the President, such as patrician social status and a Harvard education; moreover, John F. Kennedy wanted very much to defeat an incumbent Republican governor in his own home state.

The marching orders followed in rapid succession. Thomas "Tip" O'Neill, a shrewd political field general, and Kennedy's successor in his old Cambridge Congressional seat, assumed management of the Peabody campaign. Peabody then received a strong personal endorsement from the President. Eventually, the campaigns of Edward Kennedy and Endicott Peabody were combined. Common billboards, joint appearances, access to Kennedy workers and campaign donors buoyed up Peabody's bid for the governorship.

The Peabody organization now had a candidate with support, and it was going to utilize the mass media to make him identifiable in the minds of the electorate. However, it did not have any meaningful issues, and was not able to develop any. On the other hand, the opposition did have an issue, over Peabody's support of a constitutional referendum allowing the legislature to revise taxes — commonly misinterpreted as a measure to raise taxes — but it failed to exploit it.

O'Neill made a major decision on the campaign tactics to

be employed. Surveys showed that Peabody was strong in the suburban areas and weak in the Democratic cities, especially in the city of Boston. Logically, the allocation of scarce resources (the candidate's time, the workers, the billboards, etc.) could be clustered in either area. There is no political rule to dictate that resources should be concentrated in weak rather than strong areas; but O'Neill was inclined to one definite course of action:

> I moved back to my own office in Cambridge (from the Peabody headquarters staffed, in the main, by young college and professional people) where I could feel comfortable about bringing in the people I wanted to see . . . . In my district (Cambridge), we play the percentages and get out a big vote because we know that a big vote is going to yield a Democratic cushion . . . . I'd get on the telephone and call people, or we would meet and talk about the campaign . . . . I told Peabody that I would support him just so long as he was a good governor who supported his party.

O'Neill was the professional bred in urban, Democratic politics and oriented to his party rather than to abstract issues. Through highly personalized methods, he concentrated his campaign efforts on linking Peabody with the urban, Democratic vote.

A series of rallies was held in different sections of Boston, at each of which Peabody made a brief campaign speech. The objective of each was to obtain, through meetings, the support of the local leaders and their workers.

Peabody no longer appeared on his campaign charger. Instead, he attended a testimonial dinner for the controversial candidate for attorney general, Francis "Frankie" Kelly, who had been the contestant for the party's convention endorsement since the 1930's, the party maverick in the cultural mold of the urban Democratic Party. He was now tacitly endorsed by the workers' politicians in the urban core, in the presence of House Speaker John McCormack, although he had once refused to campaign for the Speaker's nephew, and had in turn been denied an appointment as district attorney of populous Middlesex County.

The political effects were cumulative. Timely campaign money entered the Peabody coffers from friends of Sheriff Fitzpatrick of Middlesex County, associates of the late governor, Paul Dever, and other political, professional, and business leaders who earlier had only contributed small amounts to Peabody.

Attempts to harm Peabody through religious smears were stopped. A facsimile of Peabody's signature on a birth control referendum was halted at its source, and its ramifications in political and clerical circles prevented. The passive resistance to Peabody's candidacy in the party's secondary ranks had been broken, and this change was conveyed to the electorate.

Reinforcing the Candidate's Appeal

Paul Lazarsfeld and his associates, in a pioneering voting study of Sandusky, Ohio, noted that the party faithfuls are activated when their latent party predispositions are reinforced by campaign materials.[9] The Peabody camp did not have the problem of activating the nominally Democratic masses in the Bay State: Edward M. Kennedy, youngest brother of the President and the U.S. Senate candidate, would bring out the vote. Of course, Peabody's candidacy did require an identification with the Democratic Party and its symbolic leader, the President of the United States. On the telephone, in film clips, and in spot announcements, the gubernatorial candidate sought these fruitful identifications:

> I am Endicott Peabody, Democratic Party candidate for governor. I am personally endorsed by our great leader,

[9] Paul F. Lazarsfeld, Bernard Berelson, and Helen Gaudet, *The People's Choice* (New York: Columbia University Press, 1944), pp. 87–93.

President John F. Kennedy, who wants me to be your governor so that we may have the same type of dynamic, progressive Democratic leadership in Massachusetts that we now enjoy in Washington.

The messages were aimed primarily at the blue-collar Democrats and their wives who lived in urban areas, people who thought that Jack Kennedy was a second Franklin Delano Roosevelt, and were enraptured by the thought of sending the President's youngest brother to the Senate of the United States.

Election Day gave proof of the wisdom of O'Neill's reinforcement strategy. In the last two weeks of the campaign, undecided Democrats, and Independents who had expressed an early preference for Governor Volpe, swung to Peabody. These changes, documented in Tables 6.8 and 6.9, reflected a shift in campaign forces.[10]

TABLE 6.8

VOTE OF UNDECIDED VOTERS IN WARD 20: BY PARTY AFFILIATION, 1962
(*Figures given as percentages*)

Candidate	*Democrats*	*Independent Democrats*	*Independent Republicans*	*Republicans*
Peabody	75	63	0	*
Volpe	25	37	100	*
Percentage of Total Undecided Vote	43	37	17	3
No. of cases	(24)	(16)	(8)	(2)

Source: *Boston College-Simmons College Political Survey.*
* Too few cases.

In 1960, Joseph Ward had had the benefit of being the candidate of the majority party, but the liabilities of his

[10] *Political Survey, op. cit.*

personality, the stereotype of a politician, and the issue he chose, of corruption among the Democrats, had led to his defeat by the Republican, John Volpe. In 1962, before the strengthening of the Democratic ranks, campaign forces were

TABLE 6.9
GUBERNATORIAL PREFERENCES IN BOSTON, WARD 20, DURING ELECTION CAMPAIGN, 1962
(*Figures given as percentages*)

	October	*November*	*Election Day*
Preference for:			
Peabody	35	41	54
Volpe	43	37	46
Undecided for:*			
Peabody	13	13	
Volpe	19	9	

Source: *Boston College-Simmons College Political Survey.*
* Based on direction of party, candidate, and issue orientations. See Angus Campbell and Others, *The American Voter* (New York: Wiley, 1960).

working against Peabody in a different way. Volpe was by now a known and approved candidate who was running against an unknown, and he was not associated with corruption. Peabody, on the other hand, was a public enigma, who was not associated with either of the two major issues, taxes and corruption, that dominate Massachusetts elections. Only the party identifications of the majority were operating in the Democrat's favor. In fact, despite the varied meaning of party association, two thirds of our Boston sample cast straight party ballots.

Peabody's favorable appearances in the mass media as a young, dynamic, and personable candidate canceled the portrait of honest John Volpe as a political personality. Moreover, Volpe's failure to link the tax tissue with Peabody erased his advantage on the campaign issues. The net result of reinforcing the favorable impression of Peabody among the Democrats was to swing the election in his favor.

E Pluribus Kennedy: The Road to Party Unity

The base of the Democratic Party, typified by the Boston Irish, returned to the fold and voted for Peabody. In 1960, Joseph Ward had received 68 per cent of the gubernatorial votes cast in the fourteen predominantly Irish wards of Boston. By reinforcing his Democratic identification, Peabody was able to secure the same percentage of the 1962 votes. Nevertheless, this was one of Peabody's poorest performances in the state: in most cities, he ran at least two percentage points ahead of Ward. However, it did provide enough footing for Peabody to defeat Governor Volpe throughout the state.

In conclusion, the nomination and election of a Democratic governor from outside the cultural mold of the majority party required access to, and control over, the party workers. If these had not participated they would probably have kept a Democrat out of the governor's chair for at least two more years. The motivating force came from the White House and from the most powerful political family in Massachusetts and in the nation, rather than from inside the Massachusetts Democratic Party. Peabody, in order to hold his loyal following of issue-oriented suburbanites, had to appear as a nonparty irregular; and yet, to muster crucial support among segments of the party regulars, he had to identify himself with the core of the Massachusetts Democratic Party, with John McCormack, with "Frankie" Kelly and his followers, and, most important of all, with the men and women in Chicopee and Charlestown who guide the voters to the polls in the teeming wards with the hope of receiving benefits from party electoral success.

This process of multiple identification is a viable political technique, but it cannot be employed continuously unless there is a more unified party apparatus willing to offer its resources to the gubernatorial candidate endorsed at the convention. Perhaps it can truly succeed only if the policy orientation of the parties and their leadership is more clearly defined in the changing political order.

CHAPTER SEVEN

PARTY POLITICS: THE REFORM DEMOCRATS

During the 1930's, the urban, immigrant groups developed political clubs to translate their political needs into reality. Three decades later, upper-middle-class suburbanites in the growing metropolitan area around Boston and Springfield developed their own political devices. COD, the Commonwealth Organization of Democrats, is an instructive example of the politics of cultural change. While it existed, it represented values basically different, and in some cases alien to the style of urban Democratic politics. More recently, Senator Edward Kennedy and State Chairman Gerald Doherty have attempted to infuse new organizational principles into a centralized Democratic Party. These events have led COD to disband because these are the goals that it has been seeking. The factors behind the formation of COD can be found in the character of the Democratic Party in 1960.

Party Reform and Effective Citizenship: The Emergence of COD

Opposition to the traditional Democratic Party came to a head in 1960 with the formation of COD by younger party members, many of them dissident state legislators dismayed by the prevailing mode of legislative politics. Many of their complaints were directed against the Democratic Speaker of the House of Representatives, John Thompson of Ludlow. Thompson's alleged violation of legislative procedures provided an issue. In addition, the lack of consistent party cohesion in the legislature and the weakness of the party's state committee concerned the reformers.

The state committee was a private creature of its chairman, John Patrick Lynch, rather than a coordinating center for Democratic electoral and governmental activities. Little effort was made to expand the party's base and to attract new voters. The fundamental political tasks of organization, campaigning, and fund raising fell to the individual candidates. Many felt that there was no Democratic electoral party, merely a collection of candidate organizations which undertook the tasks of the electoral machinery. For instance, in 1962 the party's major fund-raising affair, the Jefferson-Jackson Day dinner, was postponed by State Chairman Lynch until *after* the November election.

COD undertook to alter the base of the party structure among the emasculated executive and party leadership, legislative coteries, and electoral factions; but the organization's initial quest for identity was challenged by a suddenly active state committee chairman. Lynch contended that the insurgent group could not legally use the title "Democrat," and after a series of court battles, COD was forced to use its initials, rather than explicitly state its purpose in the name of the Commonwealth Organization of *Democrats*. Lynch's behavior was understandable, for COD sought to oust him from office and instill fresh buoyancy into the party.

"Toward a More Responsible Two-Party System"

Robert Merton, in a well-known thesis, distinguished between the overt functions of organizations and their covert functions which led to unanticipated consequences linked with the organization's operations.[1] The manifest objectives of COD were not revolutionary. Culled from the handbooks of Connecticut's John Bailey, Michigan's Neil Staebler, the reform clubs of New York and California, and the Kennedy administration (COD *Comments,* the organization's newspaper, referred to its sponsor as "the new frontier for Massachusetts Democrats"), the organization placed major stress on intraparty reforms, including a more vigorous, active, and coordinating executive committee; the reduction of nuisance challenges by recommending enactment of the Connecticut challenge primary whereby a candidate must receive at least 20 per cent of the preprimary convention votes to qualify for the party's primary; articulation of party principles in harmony with the objectives of the national party and those of the platform committee of the state party's convention; and the securing of capable candidates to run as responsible, issue-oriented men. In additon, COD sought a focal point for the party structure. The governorship was the likely post to bolster through greater administrative power, the control of party patronage, a four-year term, and enunciation of party principles and policies.

To create a more responsible two-party system and provide the electorate with a clearer choice between the "ins" and the "outs," COD urged that the governor and lieutenant governor should run on one slate, that some constitutional officials with primarily ministerial responsibilities should be appointed, instead of elected, to shorten the legacy of the Jacksonian era (the long ballot), and that the executive committee and its staff should seek to strengthen party orientation among the electorate by infusing new blood into the party and reducing the chaos of independent and split-ticket balloting.

[1] Robert K. Merton, *Social Theory and Social Structure* (Glencoe, Ill.: The Free Press, 1957), pp. 19–45.

Campaigns and Candidates

By 1962, COD had survived the prenatal stage and was ready to fight for power in statewide contests. It had recruited more than 1,000 members, having doubled its membership in less than two years. It also had a cadre headed by men with legislative experience, advisory committees composed of academic and professional specialists, a body of elected officials including eight school committeemen and four city councilors, five or six state representatives and the mayor of a growing western Massachusetts city, and local party officials — over a hundred ward and town committee members. Although it was ignored in the 1960 state convention, two years later COD was able to exert influence on the platform committee and on the behavior of the Democratic conclave. Editorial writers and political columnists of the major newspapers were useful channels for publicity: those who waged the "good fight" against corruption, even if only in print, could not help but be sympathetic to those entering the political lists under the banners of reform, progress, responsiblity, and modernization.

In the fall of 1962, COD initiated efforts to accomplish its goals by endorsing seventeen candidates for the House of Representatives in the September primaries. Next, it laid the groundwork to contest party offices in the 1962 Presidential primary, when the ward committees of 39 cities and the committees of 312 towns would be selected. Third, it made plans to introduce its measures for party and governmental reform in the legislature. Shortly before the 1963 session of the Great and General Court, a bill to establish the challenge primary was filed.

COD envisioned a grass-roots movement to restore the decaying structure of the Democratic Party, but its nominees represented the party's advance guard in suburbia. All but two of the legislative candidates endorsed by COD were either professional men or businessmen. Fifteen of the seventeen legislative districts in which candidates were endorsed were middle- to upper-middle-class suburbs, within the top 10 per cent in terms of wealth and education. Fourteen of the districts were located in the Boston metropolitan area, including three residential Boston wards; and 62 per cent of the contested legislative districts voted Republican in the 1962 gubernatorial contest.

Ten of COD's seventeen candidates, including three incumbents, won election to the lower house: all of them were from the Boston metropolitan area. Three others were unopposed in the primaries but lost in November, and the four remaining were defeated in the primaries. A close appraisal of these four contests indicates COD's range, appeal, and effectiveness.

The Democratic reform group gave top priority to the defeat of the Speaker of the House of Representatives, John Thompson. Thompson's days appeared to be numbered. In 1958, he encountered opposition in the primary for the first time in his career. In 1960, he won only after a close and bitter primary fight in his solidly Democratic district — where a primary victory is tantamount to election. A big, burly man who talked in the rhetorical style of the Al Smith era, and who called himself a "delightful rogue," Thompson was a perfect symbol of what COD wished to reform. He was a stereotype of the backroom "pol" who must "go" in the interests of party responsiblity and good government.[2]

Thompson sneered at the efforts to defeat him on the part of an organization with only a handful of members in his legislative district. His evaluation was partially correct. The COD reform ethos was not his major obstacle. Rather, two basic facts of Massachusetts politics, status and ethnic demands, challenged his reign. He was involved in a major fight to defeat Steve T. Chmura, a Ludlow businessman and representative on the regional planning committee of the Greater

[2] See *The Christian Science Monitor,* September 10, 1963, p. 2.

Springfield Citizens Committee. Chmura had trailed Thompson by only a few hundred votes in the 1960 primaries, and he lost by about the same margin in 1962. Chmura received support from his fellow Polish Americans who hoped that recognition from a prominent group representative would end control by Thompson, the Irish boss. In each election, Chmura received a majority of the votes cast in the city of Chicopee, the main enclave of Polish voters in the district, while Thompson had just enough votes in his home town of Ludlow to overcome Chmura's strength.

Thompson's support rested on his role as Speaker, a role that assured favorable consideration in the State House for the political needs of his western Massachusetts constituency. In addition, his family exerted considerable daily influence in Ludlow — his brother was city sheriff. Thus, Thompson's storehouse of political favors and patronage withstood the challenge. Nor did his political sagacity and influence fail him in another political contest. Despite the opposition of Governor-elect Peabody, new State Committee Chairman Doherty, a hand-picked spokesman of Senator Edward Kennedy, and COD, eight of whose representatives voted against the Speaker, Thompson won a sixth-ballot victory to retain his office in the 1963 session of the Massachusetts House.

COD sustained its second defeat in a Democratic stronghold when it endorsed a young social worker against the incumbent representative of a crime-ridden and poverty-stricken district in Roxbury. The incumbent, Charles Ianello, won in the pattern of his political mentor, James Michael Curley.

"Everybody in this district is on public welfare or able to get off the public welfare rolls because of Charlie," said a veteran Democrat. Charlie, the man who supplied eyeglasses and shoes to the needy, and hoped for a vote in return, had gone to prison because "they" had pinned something on him. If Charlie took a cut off the top (he was convicted for larceny of public funds), he was entitled to his commission for good works. The electorate of the Mission Hill public housing developments and of the narrow streets around Dudley Station reasoned that "they" had their cake from public and private shenanigans with the aid of high-price legal talent. In the Populist view, government was a conspiracy, and only a few practical Robin Hoods defended the interests of the common man. So, the people's choice was not a social worker but Charles Ianello.

Ianello's campaign was hurt by his temporary residence in a prison cell on Deer Island, but the "boys" carried on smartly in their candidate's absence. Six candidates of Irish extraction, whose names began with "Mc," mysteriously entered the lists against Ianello and the COD social worker, Mr. Morad. The reformer's campaign was harassed by the destruction of his literature; dubious names were entered on the voter registration list; and on election day campaigning took place within inches, rather than yards, of the polling booths.

Although Ianello failed to win a majority of the votes cast, he secured a comfortable plurality. The Parole Board saw fit to release him after he had served a few months of his three-year sentence so that he could celebrate Thanksgiving at home with his family and loyal constituents. Once more Ianello held open court for the complaints of the destitute without having to face the cries of "reform" and "constitutional revision" that came from "them."

The two other unsuccessful primary contests took place in more fruitful reform areas, a growing suburb of Springfield, and a sprawling district along Route 128 in the Boston metropolitan area. Despite the support of the mayor of Westfield in the first district and the aid of an articulate Lexington COD group in the second district, the reform candidates were again defeated by the Democratic incumbents. Each contest demonstrated the same pattern of voting: the lower-income residents of the most Democratic wards and towns outvoted the upper-income residents of the least Democratic wards and towns. The arithmetic of suburban underrepresentation still worked against the reformers. If the more affluent half of Westfield and the growing town of Lexington had been separated from their present districts, both COD candidates would have been victorious in the primary. Nevertheless, population mobility, if not prospects of legislative reapportionment, promised success to the reformers in future legislative contests along the metropolitan new frontiers.

The Managers and Their Motives

Political movements are always the handiwork of an articulate minority. Although political myths refer to government on behalf of "the people," "the general welfare," and other broad entities, the recruitment of a political minority tells us much about the objectives of political reformers. This is so because the active minority initiates or resists change.

James Q. Wilson, in an investigation of postwar Democratic reform politics in New York, Chicago, and Los Angeles, concludes that "club strength appears to be closely related to income, modified by ethnicity and status."[3] The largest concentration of reformers is found in areas with upper-income professional and business people, areas that are heavily Jewish, areas that are Republican because of income rather than status, and areas where the Democratic minority is composed of conservative, retired pensioners and lower-middle-class shopkeepers. Except for the large number of upper-status Protestants, the socioeconomic profile of COD membership, reported in Table 7.1, agrees with Wilson's findings.

The same data provide an over-all view of the areas in which COD membership has been concentrated, a view that also confirms Wilson's assessment of reform proclivities and

[3] James Q. Wilson, *The Amateur Democrats* (Chicago: The University of Chicago Press, 1962), pp. 268.

TABLE 7.1

SOCIOECONOMIC CHARACTERISTICS OF COD MEMBERSHIP
(*Figures given as percentages.* $N = 900$)

Occupation		*Sex*		*Ethnic Group*		*Religion**	
Professional	64	Male	69	Jewish	42	Jewish	42
Managerial-Business	21	Female	31	Yankee	34	Catholic	16
Sales-Clerical	13			Irish	3	Protestant and Other	42
Foreman-Craftsman	2			Italian	6		
				French	4		
				Other	11		

Source: Membership file of COD at Boston headquarters. I am grateful to Francis Meaney, former Executive Secretary of COD, for permitting me to use these data.

* Based on the classification of names in the membership files, and subject to error.

the membership of the "excluded majority," such as union members and other working-class people, and, in Massachusetts, Irish-Catholic and Italo-Catholic Democrats. (Table 7.2)

TABLE 7.2
RESIDENCE OF COD MEMBERS

Area	*Percentage of Total Membership*
Upper, Upper-Middle-Class Suburbs of Boston and Springfield	65
High Jewish Concentration	27
Upper, Upper-Middle-Class, and High Jewish or Protestant Concentration	88
Ten Largest Cities	31
Catholic, Lower-Middle and Lower-Class Areas of Ten largest Cities	8

Source: COD membership files.

An active minority, secure because it does not depend on politics for a livelihood, and buttressed with the ideology of tomorrow's reform, it is often able to thrive in one-party Republican areas where party regulars may collapse, or deteriorate into purposeless social clubs because they lack the support of party patronage and local office. However, unlike some of the New York reform clubs studied by Wilson, COD'S political strength was not concentrated in one-party Republican areas.

Indeed, COD membership was not concentrated in one-party counties or senatorial districts of either persuasion. This concentration of reformers in competitive, two-party districts stemmed from the movement of middle-income professionals of Democratic heritage to the inner and middle rings of suburbia, especially in the Boston metropolitan area, and a corresponding depletion of the older, predominantly Yankee and Republican population.

Organization: Or the Facts of Life in Politics

The political bases of COD support suggested several goals that were not set forth in the manifestos of the reform movement. First, there was the self-interest of the suburban upper-middle class. Hard pressed for fiscal resources to bolster their growing educational and property expansion, these contributors of funds, skill, and energy to the Democratic Party, underrepresented in the apportionment of legislative seats and in the party's councils, demanded a more central place in Democratic politics. Moreover, constitutional reform and extended powers for a programmatic executive, rather than power fragmented among the governmental and party notables of the core cities and small towns, best served the aims of the new managerial class.

Second, the impetus for reform came from the political ethos often associated with high status professionals and higher education, and seldom associated with the political perspectives of the excluded urban, working-class majority of the Democratic Party. The essence of this so-called "Yankee ethos," transferable to latter-day progressives among Jewish and Irish cosmopolitans, has been captured by Richard Hofstadter.

> To him (the Yankee reformer) politics was the business, the responsibility, the duty of all men. It was the arena for the realization of moral principles of broad application — and even, as in the case of temperance and vice crusades — for the correction of private habits. The immigrant, by contrast, coming as a rule from a peasant environment and from autocratic societies with strong feudal survivals, was totally unaccustomed to the active citizen's role. He expected to be acted on by government, but not to be a political agent himself. To him government meant restrictions on personal movement, the arbitrary regulation of life, the inaccessibility of the law, and the conscription of the able-bodied. To him government was the instrument of the ruling classes, characteristically acting in their interests, which were indifferent or opposed to his own. Nor was government in his eyes an affair of abstract

> principles and rules of law: it was the actions of particular men with particular powers. Political relations were not governed by abstract principles; they were profoundly personal.[4]

Hofstadter, drawing on Oscar Handlin's studies of immigrant life, is speaking of the American Progressives at the turn of the century. But his observations also apply to the electorate of Ludlow and Roxbury six decades later.

A third possible objective of reform includes the enhancement of status. Hofstadter, drawing on the work of Daniel Bell and the social psychologists, attributes Progressive motivations to anxieties about changing social status as a result of the decline of the ministry and the sudden increase in academic prestige.[5] Wilson, observing reform groups in three American cities a half century later, implies that the quest for status and the lack of fulfillment from work encourages men to enter the clubhouses of reform groups which are linked to high-status individuals such as Adlai Stevenson, Herbert Lehman, and Mrs. Eleanor Roosevelt.[6] However, there was no evidence of this motive among the Massachusetts reformers.

Instead, reform politics in Massachusetts enhanced status because it was built on prestige developed in occupational and social roles. The ranks of COD included productive scholars from the law schools and departments of political science; many were well-established professionals practicing in areas of highly rewarded specialities such as the legal aspects of missile, electronics, and space research; many were physicians, some practicing and teaching in the medical schools and public health facilities, others in medical specialities with a high degree of interpersonal contact such as psychiatry and clinical psychology; and many of the women were well-edu-

[4] Richard Hofstadter, *The Age of Reform* (New York: Knopf, 1955), p. 182.

[5] See *ibid.*, Chapter 4; Daniel Bell, *The End of Ideology* (Glencoe, Ill.: The Free Press, 1959), Chapter 6.

[6] Wilson, *op. cit.*, pp. 164–175.

cated, successful wives and mothers. Thus, positive attitudes toward work, self, and society, rather than cravings for recognition through politics, were closely linked with this reform movement.

We might conclude that reform politics is, in part, a way of offering public testimony to one's aspirations, skills, and sense of public interest. To play a successful public role in addition to a satisfying private life, this is a badge of honor worth presenting for emulation. The conversion of occupational attainment into political status is pursued by the reformers who, "accustomed as they are to success in every other sphere of life, simply do not understand how and why people like the (party) regulars come to dominate them in party offices and legislative posts."[7]

The clue to one key objective of the Massachusetts Democratic reform movement comes from Wilson's observation that "the amateur politician (one who finds politics intrinsically interesting) sees the political world more in terms of ideas and principles than in terms of persons. Politics is the determination of public policy, and public policy ought to be set deliberately rather than as the accidental by-product of a struggle for personal and party advantage."[8] This is not merely another part of the Yankee or reform ethos. It is the rational organization of public resources to accomplish public ends.

Robert Michels, writing in the ashes of his German Socialist dreams, concluded that organization and the power it produced led to oligarchy, and stifled ideology and programs.[9]

7 Daniel P. Moynihan, "Bosses and Reformers: A Profile of the New York Democrats," *Commentary, 31* (June 1961), 464–465. A useful theory of status conversion can be found in Milton M. Gordon, *Social Class in American Society* (Durham: Duke University Press, 1958), pp. 189–193, 234–256.

8 Wilson, *op. cit.*, p. 3.

9 Robert Michels, *Political Parties* (Glencoe, Ill.: The Free Press, 1949), pp. 25–36.

The COD reformers reversed his conclusion and said that organization meant progress and reform.

First, considerable unconcern about intraparty deliberation, and an excess of hierarchical decision making (decisions made by leaders being passed on to followers) were expressed in COD's objectives. There was, of course, an important structural factor, namely the absence of hierarchical power in the Democratic Party. The belief that many of the party's ills stemmed from lack of power, rather than from the actions of a heavy-handed party boss, contrasted sharply with the situation in New York — where reformers depicted Carmine DeSapio as "the Boss" in order to destroy what little real power he still possessed within a disintegrating New York Democratic Party.

Second, there was also a concern about planned decision making, utilizing skills and expertise. The private experiences of the educated professionals as reformers resulted in preferences for this type of political activity in contrast to haphazard bargaining among the regular party leaders. There was no thread of Populism in this, no attempt to destroy political machines and turn to initiative, the referendum, and the direct primary to take politics to the grass roots.

The Massachusetts reform movement was thus different from the earlier Progressive era, although the two movements did share similar social, cultural, and intellectual roots. "The central theme in Progressivism was this revolt against the industrial discipline: the Progressive movement was the complaint of the unorganized against the consequences of organization."[10] A counter organization of power was needed by the Progressives to control the dominance of big business and the trusts. The latter-day managerial progressives came, however, from the well-organized bureaucracies of scholarship, the professions, and the research industries. Rather than attempting to dilute organized power, they sought to end the

[10] Hofstadter, *op. cit.*, p. 257.

inefficiency, personal favoritism, and malingering of the public clerks in the present scheme of fragmented politics. To establish a disciplined party with executive efficiency, professional bureaucracies, and a sharper two-party choice involved breaking the personal networks which ensnared government. It is like the young second-lieutenant's effort to restore the honor of the service by curbing the power of the sergeant's NCO club in trading favors with enlisted men beyond the service manual's jurisdiction.

If this thesis of managerial reform had any merit, one would expect to see it applied to candidate preferences in Massachusetts elections. In Table 7.3, data have been assembled on four statewide elections in 1962, and on one Boston School Committee election in 1961. The preferences of areas in which COD membership comprised at least 1 per cent of the 1962 Democratic senatorial primary vote have been compared with the rest of the state.[11] The areas of COD strength supported specific candidates in each election. H. Stuart Hughes, an independent candidate for the U.S. Senate, an advocate of reciprocal initiatives leading to disarmament, and the Chairman of the Department of History and Literature at Harvard University, received more support in COD areas than elsewhere in the state.

The Republican candidate for attorney general, a well-educated, soft-spoken Negro, Edward Brooke, was also the beneficiary of support from the COD districts. Brooke's Democratic opponent was "Fighting Frankie" Kelly, a perennial

[11] Cities, towns, and Boston wards in which COD membership equaled at least 1 per cent of the total Democratic membership, as measured by the total Democratic vote in the 1962 senatorial primary contest: Boston wards 4, 5, 14, 21, 22, and the communities of Agawam, Amesbury, Amherst, Bedford, Belmont, Brookline, Chelmsford, Cohasset, Concord, Ipswich, Lexington, Lincoln, Ludlow (result of anti-Thompson campaigns), Longmeadow, Marblehead, Marshfield, Melrose, Newton, Norwood, Sharon, Sudbury, Stockbridge, Swampscott, Wayland, Wellesley, Westfield, Weston, Westwood, Williamstown, and Winchester.

TABLE 7.3

COD Areas of Strength and Voting in Five Massachusetts Elections, 1961–1962
(*Figures given as percentages*)

	*B.P.S.C. Slate, 1961**	*Hughes (I) U.S. Senator 1962*	*McCormack (D) (Primary) 1962*	*Brooke (R) Atty Gen. 1962*	*Swing Vote to Peabody, 1962 from Ward, 1960*
COD Areas of Strength	67.0	5.9	39.8	69.7	+7.9
Statewide Vote	—	2.3	31.9	56.4	+3.0
Boston Vote	51.9	—	—	—	—

Source: COD files; and 1961 and 1962 Boston and Massachusetts election returns.

* Median vote cast for four Boston Public School Committee candidates as percentage of median vote cast for eight (4, B.P.S.C.; 4, incumbents) major school committee candidates in ten-man field. Comparison of strong COD wards (4,5,14,21,22) with total Boston vote.

party maverick. Endicott Peabody, the Democratic candidate for governor and an advocate of constitutional reform and the abolition of the Executive Council, was similarly favored in the COD enclaves. These districts responded to Peabody's candidacy far more than they did to the party's aspirant in 1960, Joseph Ward.

In 1961, the declining standards of the Boston public school system produced an issue of city-wide concern. The Citizens for Boston Public Schools (C.B.P.S.) endorsed a slate of four "reform" candidates to seek places on the five-member Boston School Committee. This organization was spearheaded by young parents, who included prominent young Back Bay Republicans and COD leaders. It stressed the ineptitude of the four incumbents seeking re-election. Substantial segments of the Boston press helped the reform movement by portraying the contest as a two-party affair, essentially, between the four incumbents on the one hand and the four "reform" candidates on the other. Substantial support for the challengers in areas of COD strength helped to defeat three of the incumbents, and to elect two C.B.P.S. school committeemen.

The strong support given to Edward McCormack in upper-middle-class COD centers requires explanation in terms of the Democratic reform movement. In his unsuccessful senatorial primary contest with Edward Kennedy, Attorney General McCormack drew on a fund of good works in the fields of civil liberties and civil rights that endeared him to liberal reformers. However, advocates of pragmatic party responsiblity in academic and reform circles, including COD, argued that only Kennedy could unite the party. In the primary COD itself made no official endorsement. Then, in November, it endorsed the entire Democratic slate with the exception of Kelly, the party maverick.

The issue, whether to support Kennedy or McCormack, was hotly debated among the liberal community of the academies, COD, the fair housing practices committees, the Civil

Liberties Union, and the Americans for Democratic Action. For the first time in its history, the A.D.A. endorsed a candidate, McCormack, in the primaries on the basis of his record on civil liberties and civil rights. This was not the first time that advocates of liberalism had disagreed with the advocates of party reform. In 1960, the newly born COD engaged in a series of intramural quarrels with A.D.A. that had about as much impact on the political process as a debate between Trotskyites and Schactmanites in the plaza of Shoppers' World in Framingham.

In the long run, the strong showing of McCormack in COD strongholds can be attributed to an inversion of political stereotypes. To be sure, McCormack was a South Boston Irishman with an accent typical of the area — never a popular image for party reform — but he was seen as a competent lawyer and attorney general who had aided economic welfare through the formation of a consumer's council, and had made advances in civil liberties, civil rights, and the prosecution of corruption.

The candidacy of the President's younger brother, by contrast, was considered to be an arrogant bid for power by one with little political or professional training for the nation's highest legislative body. His candidacy was also interpreted as a sophisticated version of familial and personal politics based on connections and influence. Undoubtedly, to the managerial progressives, McCormack, not Kennedy, expressed the best hope of competent, rational politics based on achieved rather than ascribed status: his performance in a series of public acts more nearly expressed the humanistic theme of the upper-middle-class progressives.

Other data on the Democratic senatorial primary are useful in testing the thesis that the COD reform movement was an expression of status anxieties by the upwardly mobile reformers. If McCormack's support in areas of COD concentration was related to upward mobility and the uncertainty of status confirmation, one would expect to find the same pattern in other segments of the Massachusetts political community. Table 7.4 shows the relationships between social mobility and

TABLE 7.4

DEMOCRATIC SENATORIAL PRIMARY VOTE IN WEST ROXBURY (BOSTON, WARD 20), 1962: BY SOCIAL MOBILITY AMONG MIDDLE-CLASS, IRISH-CATHOLIC MALES, AGES 35–55.
(*Figures given as percentages*)

Candidate	*Upwardly Mobile Middle Class**	*Status-Constant Middle Class†*
Kennedy	72	54
McCormack	28	46
No. of Cases	(74)	(43)

Source: *Boston College-Simmons College Political Survey.*
* Middle-class sons of working-class fathers.
† Middle-class sons of middle-class fathers. Social class defined by occupation, with professional, proprietary, managerial, sales, and clerical pursuits classified as middle class.

senatorial primary preferences among the residents of a mobile middle-class, Irish-Catholic ward, when party affiliation, age, sex, ethnicity, religious affiliation, and residence are controlled. The middle-class sons of working-class fathers are more likely to vote for Kennedy than the middle-class sons of middle-class fathers. The upwardly mobile man is caught between two sets of political values: the public premises of the bourgeoisie that he is entering, and the assumptions of his working-class background. The Kennedys are a status symbol for the aspiring middle class of their native Commonwealth, especially for those of Irish-Catholic extraction. They epitomize the material and social success to which the new middle class aspires. At the same time, the attachment is highly personal and familial, reflecting the shared tribal loyalties that mark the immigrant-derived world of political bargaining. Here, then, is the material to mold working-class bases of political allegiance with middle-class aspirations of wealth and status.

The support of the COD Democrats for Hughes, Peabody, McCormack, Brooke, and the C.B.P.S. candidates reflected more than a single motivating force. First, there was a common humanitarian liberalism in supporting candidates who espoused peace, constitutional revision, civil liberties, civil rights, and better education. Second, there were overlapping group memberships that found COD members active in the A.D.A., the C.B.P.S., the fair housing committees, and the American Civil Liberties Union. Third, there was a preference for wordly, cosmopolitan candidates over the parochial men immersed in the smaller, local orbit.[12] Volpe, the hod-carrier and contractor, Francis Kelly, the open-door lawyer of the common man, the members of the Boston School Committee with their limited horizons of educational policy, and even Edward Kennedy, seen in the familial hues already sketched, did not capture the imagination of those whose cultural equipment linked them with the new Democrats.

In addition, the practical need to attract political support in Massachusetts reinforced the belief that a rational mode of politics should, essentially, be based on organizational premises. Only about 20 per cent of the COD membership was either Catholic, Irish, or Italian. No political movement, especially an internal movement in the Massachusetts Democratic Party, can hope to attract more than regional support unless it can appeal to the growing Catholic, ethnic subcommunities attaining managerial rank. The impetus for party and governmental reform, rather than civil liberties and disarmament, gained strength as it was imparted to these growing segments which shared the socioeconomic position of most COD members. The organization of COD indicated an attempt to bolster its strength in precisely these segments of the party. Although Catholics comprised only about one-fifth of the membership, 40 per cent of COD's board of directors, about half of its candidates for state representative in 1962, and most of the

[12] Merton, *op. cit.*, pp. 387–420.

regional leaders were Catholic, predominantly of Irish extraction.

The Prospects for Reform

There were, to be sure, vast potential differences between COD, its fellow travelers in the electorate, and the mainstream of party regulars. These differences were accentuated by the gulf between the ethos of civic duty and the political style of material reward and personal relationship. Nevertheless, in a larger sense, the middle-class ethos of reform and good government has not seriously been challenged for primacy among sociopolitical symbols. There is no autonomous working-class political culture in American society, just as there is no major alternative ethnic, religious, or ideological culture. Rather, the general ethos of managerial reform exists alongside numerous other particular interests, and often they all operate through distinct public channels. Thus, many objectives of potential conflict are ignored by one group or the other.

The politically interesting developments in reform politics occur when they are brought into broad party and governmental forums, for it is then that political conflicts develop. The entry of the professional middle class into politics through such phenomena as the Stevenson campaigns and their aftermath has less been a search for status than an attempt at political socialization. It has been an attempt to acculturate the excluded majority to the styles of the managerial, bureaucratic world outside the neighborhood, the parish, and the shop. When these attempts have been resisted, as they often have, efforts have been observed not solely of reform but of political integration.

In Massachusetts, the central function of reform has been to make contact with the national administration, the national Democratic Party, and the technical, economic, scientific, and administrative problems with which they grapple. Since the managers' resources include mobility and skills, it would be remarkable if they did not serve as useful allies for those in the larger world of national and international politics who seek to implement policy decisions. Whatever its programmatic baggage (medical care, tax reform, support of the United Nations), this is essentially an administrative concept of government that resembles the theories of public-administration textbooks between 1920 and 1945. Rationality, responsibility, belief in the progress motif, and efficiency are stressed by the Hamiltonian Democrats seeking to integrate a party so that it may better serve their state and national purposes.

In essence, the COD reform movement, now linked with a revitalized Democratic Party executive committee and chairman, operates under the umbrella of managerial progressivism. The managerial progressives serve as a cadre of political middlemen between the local Massachusetts polity and the broader political world of Washington and Whitehall. The reformers appear to occupy a tangential, although increasingly influential, position in relation to the self-contained political system in Massachusetts. From the broader perspective of the American political system, COD has served as a communications center between national elites and the local party's leaders and followers.

This interpretive function necessitates an ability to establish rapport with many groups: this is a skill the lawyers, physicians, and academics who belonged to COD manifested in their professional lives.[13] Good government and the rationale of reform do not necessarily harmonize with this mediating function. It is in this sense that the pragmatic and ideological objectives of the reform movement may conflict. So long as their professional and cultural base suggests

[13] In 1963 a COD charter member and state representative from the Boston suburbs was elected to fill a vacancy on the Democratic State Committee without a single dissenting vote, but some setbacks were suffered in 1964.

alternative public policies, the managerial progressives are likely to conflict with the Democratic majority. This result may, in turn, seriously impair the reformers' ability to serve as connecting links between the parochial and cosmopolitan political worlds.[14]

By the spring of 1964, the COD organization had decided to dissolve and to merge with the newly organized party machinery controlled by the Kennedys. Its statistical accomplishments had been impressive: its members were on at least fifty-five city and town committees, and held chairmanships in a dozen local organizations; and there were six COD-endorsed candidates elected to the Democratic State Committee. It had unified more than 1,500 reform-minded Democrats, but the long-term significance of COD's efforts lay in its attempt to create a rational and managerial political party.

[14] Consult the excellent critique of reform politics and the functions of political parties in Wilson, *op. cit.*, pp. 340–370.

PART IV

POLITICAL INSTITUTIONS *AND PUBLIC POLICIES*

CHAPTER EIGHT

MAKING STATE GOVERNMENT WORK

Massachusetts government is highly decentralized with powers and functions widely dispersed among an array of official and informal groups. More importantly, the governmental structure is closely affected by the legacy of political demands made upon it by the Yankee Brahmins, the urban immigrant groups, and more recently, the new managerial classes with their penchant for reform and consolidation. Thus, the legislature and the Executive Council provide the major avenues of urban political control.

The Difficulty of Divided Government

The problems of divided government are very clearly visible in the Bay State and it is, therefore, useful to begin with them. The governor has always been elected for a two-year term, which means that he has about one year in which to become acquainted with governmental processes and a second year in which to begin campaigning again. Therefore, he has seldom been able to exert enough leverage over the system to make major policy or administrative innovations. Moreover, the governor and lieutenant governor have not run as a team; instead, they have constituted a divided executive, even when both have been elected from the same party. For instance, in 1964, Lieutenant Governor Francis Bellotti declared his gubernatorial candidacy against his fellow Democrat and 1962 running mate, Governor Endicott Peabody. Bellotti had used his office as an alternate decison-making center for those groups and individuals excluded from the governor's inner circle. The division of power and function is accentuated by the election of such essentially ministerial offices as state treasurer, state auditor, and secretary of state, as well as that of attorney general. Thus, each officeholder musters his own support during elections, and attempts to fashion a quasi-autonomous position during his term in office.

Also significant is the board and commission system, a heritage of the belief that policy positions should be insulated from "politics." This places many individuals whose terms overlap with that of the governor in positions of authority during the term of his successor. It also means that an outgoing governor may trade a backlog of appointments to acquire support. This weakens the patronage power of the incoming governor and, in turn, his ability to achieve the major aspects of his program. For instance, in 1960, Governor Volpe, with the approval of the Executive Council, filled all but four judgeships shortly before leaving office. Governor Peabody was, thus, deprived of important bargaining power during his first months in office. The Executive Council, an archaic institution designed originally to check the powers of the colonial royal governor, acts as a major tollgate keeper, since the governor must obtain its approval in filling over eight hundred major and minor positions.

The effects of this fragmented executive power on the state administration are clear. It is almost a misnomer to speak of governmental bureaucracies in Massachusetts, since the term connotes disciplined levels of professional staffs working under unified direction. It is more typical to find policy and patronage favoritism. It exists among a wide array of cliques including members of state agencies, interest groups, and elected legislative and executive positions. With the notable exception of a few departments such as Public Health and Mental Health, there is little professional policy orientation in the operation of state government. The old notion that a state job brings security or the opportunity for enrichment to depressed immigrant-group members still exerts great pressure on the operation of public functions. Moreover, considerable administrative power is vested in quasi-autonomous commissions and authorities on the theory that this status removes them from gubernatorial politics and gives them the requisite governmental authority. In fact, this theory and the power of individuals such as the late William Callahan, Chairman of the Massachusetts Turnpike Authority, make it difficult for the governor or the legislature to reclaim supervisory powers over the operation of special authorities. It was, for instance, only under the greatest public pressure that the Great and General Court voted in 1962 that the Turnpike Authority should make its financial records available for independent public audit.

The legislative branch also functions under the premise that divided authority and frequent elections ensure governmental responsiveness to the citizenry. The bicameral Great and General Court stands for election every two years. Although there have been innovations such as joint committees, which avoid legislative duplication, the normal tendency is toward an array of committees, a heritage of the town meeting era that required all citizen petitions to receive committee and floor consideration.

Students of administrative efficiency who believe in strong governors, elected for four-year terms with powers commensurate with their responsibility, are frustrated by the fragmented nature of the Massachusetts polity. The institutionally weak governor, the plural executives, the seemingly endless biennial elections of all elected officials, the absence of a merited, professional bureaucracy and state civil service, and the old powers of the Executive Council, unresponsive to a short-term governor — all these are products of successive group demands on government resulting in a system of political veto where provisions inimical to interests may be amended or deleted.

Policy Making and the Veto Groups

A state that is economically and politically diverse is unlikely to be under the control of a clearly defined and powerful minority with commanding influence on most major political decisions. Conjecture is not evidence, however, so it is instructive to examine certain decisions that were noted by students of Massachusetts politics for the period from 1946 to 1963.[1]

LABOR-MANAGEMENT

1949 Restrictive labor legislation proposed by Republican Governor Bradford. Supported by Greater Boston Chamber of Commerce (C.C.), Associated Industries of Massachusetts (A.I.M.), about half the Republican legislators, and the Massachusetts Federation of Taxpayers' Associations (F.T.A.). *Opposed and defeated* by AFL-CIO, Americans for Democratic Action (A.D.A.), and 80 per cent of the Democratic legislators.

1960 Bill requiring registration of imported strikebreakers. *Supported and passed* by AFL-CIO with support from the same groups and opposition from the same groups as listed above.

PUBLIC WELFARE, BENEFITS

1957 Bill providing unemployment compensation after six weeks to strikers. Initiated by AFL-CIO with support

[1] See Duane Lockard, *New England State Politics* (Princeton: Princeton University Press, 1959); Murray B. Levin and George Blackwood, *The Compleat Politician: Political Strategy in Massachusetts* (Indianapolis: Bobbs-Merrill, 1962); John H. Fenton, *The Catholic Vote* (New Orleans: The Hauser Press, 1960).

of A.D.A. and a slim majority of Democratic legislators. *Opposed and defeated* by C.C., A.I.M., F.T.A., sizable minority of Democrats, and large majority of Republican legislators.

1949 State-operated compulsory sickness-insurance plan proposed by Democratic Governor Dever with support of most Democrats, AFL-CIO, A.D.A. *Opposed and defeated* by insurance interests, large majority of Republicans, and significant minority of Democrats.

PARTY AS INTEREST GROUP

1952 Dever proposes new state jobs, pensions, allowances at end of legislative session. *Opposed and defeated* by F.T.A. with votes of solid Republican majority and significant Democratic minority.

1962 William Callahan, Chairman of Massachusetts Turnpike Authority, seeks bill permitting turnpike development in Boston to be exempt from Boston zoning and other regulations. Supported by large majority of Democrats and significant Republican minority, and A.I.M. *Opposed and defeated* by veto of Governor Volpe (Republican), who was supported by Boston's Mayor Collins, business and financial interests, and the *Boston Herald Traveler*, as well.

HOME RULE

1961 Boston mayor given right to appoint Boston police commissioner. *Supported and initiated* by Mayor Collins, and the Boston Democratic delegation. Unsuccessfully opposed by most outstate Republicans and some outstate Democrats.

CHURCH AND STATE

1959 John Powers *defeated* in Boston mayoral contest despite support from prominent clergymen in Boston Archdiocese.

1958 Planned Parenthood League *opposed and defeated* in birth control referendum by Catholic Church, with socioeconomic and religous factors evident in voting patterns.

1962 Attempts to extend Day of Rest exemptions to Sabbatarians initiated by segments of the Jewish community, Seventh Day Adventists, Catholic legislative leaders, and the American Civil Liberties Union. *Opposed and defeated* by Catholic Church, its lay organizations, and the Lord's Day League of Massachusetts. On reconsideration, most Protestant Republicans in favor and most Catholic Democrats opposed to exemptions.

TAXATION

1951 Small income tax increase *initiated and passed* by Governor Dever. Supported by A.D.A., most Democrats and labor organizations, and opposed by C.C., F.T.A., A.I.M., business and financial community, and *Boston Herald Traveler*. Dever was defeated in 1952: the tax increase was an element in the voting behavior of the new expanding suburban middle classes.

1956 More nearly graduated income tax proposed by Democratic leaders with support of League of Women Voters of Massachusetts and A.D.A. *Opposed and defeated* on sharp party vote with 3 per cent of Republicans joining Democratic majority, while 8 per cent of Democrats joined Republican minority. This outcome prevented absolute majority required for passage of constitutional amendment. C.C. and F.T.A. led interest groups opposing amendment.

1957 Sales tax proposed by Democratic Governor Foster Furcolo, received moderate and varying support from financial and business community, Massachusetts Teachers Association, A.I.M., *Boston Herald Traveler,* F.T.A., State and Local Employees' Union and other labor groups. Measure opposed by many unions and union leaders, A.D.A., small-town Republican and core-city Democratic legislative leaders, and the Massachusetts Retail Druggists' and Retail Grocers' Association. Measure *opposed and defeated* as 47 per cent of the Democratic legislators joined 65 per cent of the Republicans.

1962 Referendum to give legislature broader taxing power including consideration of graduated income and other tax measures. *Opposed and defeated* by four-to-one vote of electorate, a result advocated by the F.T.A. and some labor locals. Measure supported by executive committee of AFL-CIO and by League of Women Voters.

James Madison would not have been dismayed by the play of social checks and balances, although Hamilton and Jefferson might have differed. In no area of decision making does a single interest consistently get its way: at least two interest groups are involved in every decision, and no particular group participates in every decision.

Moreover, intensive studies of each decision reveal a delicate series of negotiations in which participants are given a meaningful hearing. In ten of the fourteen cases, the power of political veto was successfully exercised to protect a group's base values. Labor defeated restrictive legislation; the Catholic Church defeated birth control proposals that ran counter to its basic moral code; and the late Mr. Callahan of the Turnpike Authority was defeated, despite his enormous power, when he tried to intrude on the base values of Boston's administration.

It is highly improbable that any group can either be severely deprived itself or deprive other groups of fundamental values. In this politics of moderation, it is unlikely that the clamor of extreme movements, led by politically deprived men, will seriously affect broad public policies.

However, new proposals may not be heard above group demands for the protection of political interests often attained after decades of struggle. In fortresses protected by deep moats, labor resists unregistered strikebreakers, the Catholic Church the legislation of birth control, and the insurance industry the establishment of "socialized insurance." Only foolhardy political squires would attempt to storm these fortresses. However, the knight who hopes to guide the political system finds that his path cannot remain in the open fields but must cross the moats of some established interests.

Thus, a winning coalition cannot be forged behind a tax policy that seeks to increase revenues to meet the growing needs of metropolitan areas. Neither interest-group nor party unity can muster enough power to alter tax policies substantially. With political leadership divided, it is not surprising that a referendum passed on to the people failed to alleviate the problem. This failure was cleverly encouraged by the conservative spokesmen of the Federated Taxpayers' Alliance who implied that the measure to give taxing powers to the legislature contained in fact a graduated tax.

In short, the way in which Massachusetts public policy is formulated prevents minority rule, but enhances minority veto. Minority enrichment, whether exercised by state employees, contractors, or the underworld is bound to be discovered, vocalized, and made a political issue, thus increasing the likelihood that small-group political monopolies in dark corners of the governmental apparatus will encounter antitrust measures.

These tendencies are increased by the diversity and size of key interest groups. When the AFL-CIO conflicts with the A.I.M. and the N.A.M. the competitors before the public are each powerful and visible. The socioeconomic structure of Massachusetts lacks such primary economic antagonists as the U.A.W. and the automobile industry in Michigan. Instead, the major fiscal, commercial, labor, and educational interests in the Bay State have to go to Washington to initiate significant political pressures or to reverse "lower-court rulings" by an arm of state government.

Those interest groups most dependent on state and local political resources and political outcomes are the small buyers and sellers of influence. Their operations resemble family capitalism rather than industrial monopoly. Like fluid factions in a weak party system, these shifting bands of public employees, small business and labor groups, contractors, liquor, dog-racing, and horse-racing interests press their demands through both party systems and in all state governmental institutions. The result is to fragment still further the political structure, erase party and ideological differences, and, most important, reinforce the characteristic patterns of personalized bartering. It is this tendency, caused in large measure by forces in the political economy beyond the state boundaries, that breeds the new politics of the four cultures already described.

Crossing Party Lines: Fiscal Policy

While party divisions are important in Massachusetts government, two matters of major public concern, namely fiscal policy and legislative political leadership, are increasingly influenced by the divergent cultural bases in Massachusetts and are creating political coalitions across party lines.[2] The effect of partisanship on the formation of legislative policies will be examined first and then the cultural ramifications of legislative leadership.

The Massachusetts legislature traditionally has a high voting record, which reflects internal party cohesion and external party differences. One study found that Massachusetts ranked second to Pennsylvania in legislative party cohesiveness among thirteen northern states examined for selected years between 1931 and 1959.[3] In addition, in the New England

[2] Malcolm E. Jewell, "Party Voting in American State Legislatures," *American Political Science Review, XLIX* (September 1955), 773–791.

[3] Malcolm E. Jewell, *The State Legislature* (New York: Random House, 1962), pp. 49–55.

states the distribution of political rewards and costs is directly related to the degree of party competition. Business interests bear a greater share of the tax load, and deprived groups receive greater per capita benefits, as in aid to the blind, the disabled, the aged, and dependent children. Antidiscrimination laws in employment have wider application in Massachusetts than they do in New Hampshire. This latter state, with comparable socioeconomic characteristics, has a one-party system that ensures rural and Republican legislative control, and that increases internal Democratic disorganization.[4] Although other nonparty factors are probably in operation, the link between electoral and governmental party systems is evident in public policy.

There are, of course, demographic and structural reasons for the general importance of party in Bay State decision making. Differences in social class reinforced by ethnic, regional, and religious variations increase the likelihood that a lower-level, Irish-Catholic, and Boston corps of legislators will unite in opposition to an upper-level, Yankee-Protestant, and outstate Republican group. The traditional power of the House Speaker, the utilization of joint legislative committees that prevent greater fragmentation of power, the requirement that bills must be reported out of committee, and the absence of provisions requiring a roll call on every measure brought to the floor, probably increase the salience of party on legislative output.

However, it is useful to divide state public policy into six categories — party welfare, public welfare, labor-management relations, home rule or local control, civil liberties, and civil rights and related measures — to indicate how party varies in legislative decisions.

In Massachusetts and most other states the level of party cohesion is highest on matters affecting the party apparatus as an interest group; although, as indicated below, recent

[4] Lockard, *op. cit.,* pp. 326–337.

conflicts over the office of Speaker suggest basic changes in Massachusetts politics. Issues involving elections, reapportionment, the civil service, state administration, and legislative organization and procedure usually result in party votes. The specific decisions listed and discussed above indicate that labor-management relations are also a customary source of division between the parties.

Labor-management disputes have accounted for 20.2 per cent of party roll calls in Massachusetts, but for only 11.4 per cent of party roll calls in eight other two-party states during comparable periods examined.[5] To be sure, minority or majority legislative status affects cohesion, but there is greatest Democratic unity on issues that affect the basic values of labor over time. Urban and suburban Republicans often avoid positions that are against collective bargaining and union-shop agreements.

In general, public welfare items produce a moderate rate of interparty schism and intraparty disagreement. In fact, welfare, health, and education issues accounted for only 4.5 per cent of all party disputes in Massachusetts that were examined by one scholar, compared with 13.6 per cent of the party disputes considered in eight other two-party states. Obviously, many Republicans are voting for welfare measures in highly urban states. In some matters, especially education, the lack of party cohesion is due to splits between the two major elements of each party.

The pressures of educational expansion are most keenly felt in the metropolitan suburbs with their large numbers of young children, high educational expectations beyond high school, relatively low concentration of school children in parochial schools, and the high value put on education by professional and business, college-educated parents. These forces are weakest in the core cities and small towns. There-

[5] The discussion of party issues is based on data in Lockard, *op. cit.*, p. 154; Jewell, "Party Voting in American State Legislatures," *op. cit.*, pp. 788–790.

fore, it is common for suburban Democrats and suburban Republicans to initiate and support education bills. It is also common for fiscally conservative small-town yeomanry and workers' politicians covertly to oppose these measures in committee and on the floor: no one can be openly against education in American society. If any discernible voting patterns materialize, public expenditures for roads, highways, and health clinics are more likely to reveal interparty schism.

Historically, disputes over local issues occupy a relatively large part of the party legislative agenda. The studies cited indicate that local matters accounted for only 2.6 per cent of party disputes in eight state legislatures, as against 16.8 per cent of such schisms in the Great and General Court. These involve debates between Boston Democrats and outstate Republicans over the degree of political autonomy and power to be awarded the Hub.

Increasingly, small-town Republicans and Boston Democratic legislators share attitudes on state-local relations. The yeomen voted against Foster Furcolo's sales tax despite considerable pressures from the Boston commercial community and the Republican Party's patrician leadership, and the inducement of aid to the cities and towns in exchange for support. In 1963, conflict-of-interest provisions separating remunerative services to town government and official participation in town government were bitterly opposed by many selectmen and their state representatives.

Lack of interest in broad state government and exaggerated localism have their urban Democratic counterparts. As Mallan and Blackwood indicate:

> While all Massachusetts legislators work to obtain funds for their districts for such projects as roads and public works, few seem to think of themselves as "ambassadors," like those in Congress and other state legislatures, dedicated to obtaining large-scale state aid for their districts or helping to keep down local taxes. Instead, the state legislature frequently votes to add to the costs of local government by such devices as raising the state minimums for salaries paid to local employees

without providing state funds, or giving life tenure to particular local employees and groups of employees. *This practice of what may be called "anti-aid" — adding to the costs of government in their own areas — is especially prevalent in legislation relating to Boston and other large cities.*[6]

In both cases, yeomen Republicans and urban Democratic representatives unite in defense of local versions of the "states' rights" thesis.

Varying attitudes toward civil liberties are more difficult to locate in legislative roll calls. As is often the case, crucial decisions are reached off the legislative floor or in other places such as the governor's and the attorney general's offices. In fact, the supporters of civil liberties are highly concentrated in the academic, professional, and suburban enclaves on the outskirts of the Boston and Springfield metropolitan areas, and it is suburban legislators who often officially initiate fair-housing measures, strengthen civil-rights provisions, and curb tendencies to witch hunt that have possessed some public officials from the old Massachusetts Bay Colony to the present Commonwealth.

It is in the area of fiscal accumulation and disbursement that the parties and their leaders are least effective as molders of legislative opinion. It has been found, for example, that "taxation and appropriations together gave rise to a large number of votes in all of the (eight two-party) states examined except Massachusetts. These issues might be expected to cause a high level of party voting in all states, since they are essential to the prestige and success of any administration. *In the four urban states other than Massachusetts, these two issues resulted in a high level of party voting.*"[7] Democrats are more likely to support progressive taxation, while Repub-

[6] John P. Mallan and George Blackwood, "The Tax That Beat a Governor: The Ordeal of Massachusetts," in *The Uses of Power,* edited by Alan F. Westin (New York: Harcourt, Brace and World, 1962), p. 306 (italics mine).

[7] Jewell, "Party Voting in American State Legislatures," *op. cit.,* p. 789 (italics mine).

licans are more likely to advocate regressive tax measures such as the sales tax. However, there is no general agreement within either party on the best methods to increase state revenues and allocations substantially.

The absence of consensus on fiscal policy cannot be attributed solely to a fear of retribution at the polls on the part of a public that wants the benefits of government without paying its costs. One explanation is that representatives from districts typical of their party and with wide election margins tend to show the highest degree of party loyalty in legislative roll calls.[8] However, this was true only in the session of 1931–1932 when the party cohesion of Democrats was ascertained by a set of ten roll calls *mostly on labor issues,* and in 1941 when deviations from party positions were measured by an index tabulated by the Massachusetts Federation of Labor. A new feaure "appears in 1951 (in) the behavior of Democrats with wide election margins. Previously they tended slightly more toward party regularity than did their party colleagues with narrow margins. In 1951, they tended to diverge more from their party."[9] The reason was the presence of Governor Dever's income-tax measure and other revenue legislation which reduced internal Democratic agreement. Similarly, Republican discipline declines as one moves from party and management claims to welfare measures and to basic fiscal policies. An analysis of Senator Saltonstall's vote between 1947 and 1954 indicates that by AFL-CIO standards "he cast his 'right' votes on questions of social welfare and domestic economic policy, not on labor matters."[10]

Except on such measures as unemployment benefits and

[8] Duncan MacRae, Jr., "The Relation Between Roll Call Votes and Constituencies in the Massachusetts House of Representatives," *American Political Science Review, XLVI* (December 1952), 1046–1055.

[9] *Ibid.,* p. 1052.

[10] Lockard, *op. cit.,* p. 145.

labor-management relations, cultural differences are more important than party divisions. This proposition can be substantiated by an analysis of fifteen key roll calls during the 1963–1964 session of the General Court which were examined by the Americans for Democratic Action. On five economic issues, involving the Consumers' Council and salaries and unemployment benefits, party cleavage was dominant. On ten other cultural and administrative issues, ranging from discrimination in housing and transportation to reorganization of the Department of Public Works and limitations on the statutory powers of the Executive Council, core-city Democrats and small-town Republicans voted against the "reform" proposals supported by the suburban wing of each party. Seven or more of these ten non-welfare measures were supported by 49 per cent of the suburban Democrats, 50 per cent of the suburban Republicans, 20 per cent of the core-city Democrats, and 20 per cent of the small-town Republicans.

One reason for the absence of party cleavage on fiscal and other matters can be discovered through a comparison of the occupational characteristics of legislators in Massachusetts with those in other urban, two-party states. This has been done using an index of interparty class differences: legislators with professional occupations are given a score of 3; business-managerial, 2; sales-clerical, 1; and blue-collar, 0; the totals are then divided by the number of legislators for each party.[11] It can be seen, in Table 8.1, that occupational differences between the legislative parties are least in Massachusetts.

In the Bay State, in contrast to Michigan and Pennsylvania, there are few union members or officials in the Democratic legislative ranks. The main support for many senior Democratic legislators, especially those from parts of Boston, rests on the small property owners, sales-clerical and skilled

[11] V. O. Key, Jr., *American State Politics* (New York: Knopf, 1956), pp. 259–262.

TABLE 8.1

INDICES OF INTERPARTY SOCIAL-CLASS DIFFERENCES IN THREE STATE LEGISLATURES

State	*Indices**	*Percentage of Legislators Included†*
Massachusetts	0.22	87.5
Michigan	1.90	76.1
Pennsylvania	1.95	82.2

Source: Data compiled from V. O. Key, Jr., *American State Politics*, pp. 259–262, for the 1945, 1947, 1949, and 1951 sessions.

* See text for explanation of indices. If all Republicans in a legislature were professional men and all Democrats were blue-collar workers, the index of class differences would be 3.00. If all legislators of both parties were usually employed as salesmen or clerks, for instance, the index would be 0.00.

† Excludes legislators whose occupations did not fall into one of four major categories, e.g., farmers.

workers, and the general lower-middle class, rather than on the mass industry, blue-collar base.

Although party and interest-group differences have an impact on the distribution of fiscal benefits and costs in Massachusetts, cultural values play an even more fundamental role in formulating finance policy. Any redistribution of costs through a sales tax or graduated income tax is most threatening to the declining centers of population and wealth in the state, namely the core cities and small towns. At the same time, the major demands for new educational and other public benefits arise in the metropolitan fringes because of their growing and relatively young population.

At one time, basic policies on state finances were used essentially as devices through which rural Republicans from western Massachusetts could hinder the central city needs of Boston, and to a lesser extent, of other major population centers. Although some of these restrictions persist, both the core cities and the small towns, and the worker and yeoman ideologies that they nourish, now combat changes in fiscal policy that would, for instance, increase state aid to education and benefits to property owners in the suburban developments. The reason for this is that the costs of these benefits are passed on to the core cities and small towns. All politics involves coalitions designed to contest particular policies, and long-term legislative alignments on fiscal matters suggest that the core-city and rural legislators use their strategic dominance in the Great and General Court to block substantial alterations in the distribution of costs and benefits in the state.

Bipartisan Leadership and the Suburban Revolt

In the period before the New Deal, the patrician-yeoman Republican alliance used the speakership and other leadership positions to defend moderately conservative economic policies. During the following decades, the urban Democrats acquired power and legislative hegemony. Determinations of legislative leadership in the 1960's reflect the values and power positions of the workers' politicians from the core cities, the managers and patricians from the suburbs, and the yeomen from the small towns.

In the first place, the growing suburban areas of Massachusetts are underrepresented in the state legislature. By contrast, the core-city delegations from Boston and elsewhere are the most overrepresented on the basis of population. Note in Table 8.2 the disparities in voting strength that are found in Massachusetts, in all state legislatures, and even in the U.S. House of Representatives. While redistricting may alter these distributions somewhat, the majority Democratic Party includes a disproportionate number of senior men from the core cities who reinforce the institutional conservatism of the party's legislative wing. They are complemented by the dominant legislative wing of the Republican Party from the small towns and hamlets. Therefore, representatives on the frontiers of two-party competition — in

TABLE 8.2

CURRENT MALAPPORTIONMENT IN DIFFERENT LEGISLATIVE SYSTEMS

	Type of Constituency		
	Urban	*Suburban*	*Rural*
U.S. House of Representatives	95*	75	112
Massachusetts General Court	130	78	117
All State Legislatures	76	50	171

Source: Congressional and state legislative data taken from *The Politics of Reapportionment,* edited by Malcolm E. Jewell (New York: Atherton Press, 1962), pp. 18–23; Paul T. David and Ralph Eisenberg, *Devaluation of the Urban and Suburban Vote* (Charlottesville: Bureau of Public Administration, University of Virginia, 1961), pp. 8–16.

* Denotes weight of vote. In an ideally apportioned political system all votes would be worth 100. If this were true in Massachusetts the rural areas would lose five seats, the urban areas fifteen seats, and the suburban districts would gain twenty seats. The Boston delegation in the lower house is the main source of malapportionment. Redistricting according to registered voters would cut the Boston delegation in half.

the inner suburbs of the Boston metropolitan area, for instance — speak for the politically deprived Republican and Democratic suburban voters in the Great and General Court.

In 1963, three of the four party groupings in the legislature engaged in controversy over their leadership. Only John E. Powers, Democratic President of the Senate, won the united support of his party. On the Republican side of the aisle, Minority Leader Fred Lamson was deposed by Senator Phillip Graham who urged a more aggressive Republican strategy and program in the upper chamber. The outcome was affected by the characteristics of the political constituencies and the legislators. While two of the three Republican senators from generally middle-class suburban districts supported Graham, three of the five senators from predominantly rural, small-town districts voted for Lamson. Graham secured the deciding votes of the two Republican senators from urban districts, including Senator Ames from Boston's Back Bay. His district closely approximates the metropolitan-fringe suburbs in the occupational, educational, and political characteristics of its constituents. Moreover, the days of the Cabots, the Lodges, and the Deity are passed, and the Back Bay district now has considerable two-party competition.

On the Republican side of the House of Representatives, Minority Leader Sidney Curtis, former moderator of the town meeting in a Berkshire village, was hard pressed by David Locke of Wellesley, spokesman for an affluent community in burgeoning Norfolk County. Curtis, retaining his post after a secret ballot at a Republican caucus, promised more say to the disgruntled minority. All three of Locke's lieutenants came from suburban constituencies, while four of Curtis' five prominent supporters came from hamlets socially compatible with his native Sheffield.

The major leadership fight centered around the office of Speaker of the House, currently held by a Democrat, John Thompson of Ludlow. Thompson had barely won his primary fight against a prominent Polish businessman supported by COD. Initially, opposition to Thompson clustered around Michael Paul Feeney, leader of a residential Boston ward and a key supporter of the newly elected Democratic Governor Endicott Peabody at the preprimary nominating convention. Peabody reciprocated by supporting Feeney against his own incumbent Speaker.

In an effort to obtain the outstate support necessary to block Thompson's re-election, the bulk of the anti-Thompson vote swung to a representative from Lowell. When the roll call began, Thompson's opponents hoped that Senator-elect Edward M. Kennedy would drop from the skies like a young Jonathan Edwards to vent his wrath on those who had swayed from the new orthodoxy of middle-class respectability to support Thompson, a self-styled "delightful rogue." Kennedy, however, was busy in Washington. With the aid of Republican votes and Republican support in the form of convenient absences, Thompson secured the majority of the representatives on the sixth ballot. The remaining ballots were distributed among House Minority Leader Curtis, Kiernan of Lowell, Feeney, and two other Democrats. Years of legislative power and reciprocity had withstood the opposition of a new governor and the implicit desires of a new United States senator.

Despite his origins in western Massachusetts, Thompson's strongest support came from the Boston Democratic delegation, especially the representatives from low-income wards. More generally, his Democratic support came from less affluent Catholic minority groups (the Italian, Polish, French, and Portuguese Americans) who voted for Thompson by a margin of four to one. This contrasts with the support he received from 62 per cent of all Irish Democrats, who tend to come from more affluent districts, and from 67 per cent of all Democrats in the lower house. His strongest opposition came from the Boston Republicans whose constituencies, concentrated in the Back Bay, most resemble the metropolitan suburbs of Boston and Springfield. With party held constant, there was a progressive decline in support for Thompson as one moved from the cities to the small towns, and from there to the suburbs.

Large numbers of suburban and Boston Republicans shifted from an intermediary position to register a strong protest against Thompson and, indirectly, against their own yeoman leadership by voting for one of the Democrats. On the other hand, the small-town and rural core of Republican legislators, who receive the lion's share of the party's seniority and committee rewards, showed the highest index of support for Thompson of any Republican sociopolitical grouping.

The two deviant groupings, rural Democrats and urban Republicans, occupied moderate positions. In summary, a coalition of core-city Democrats and small-town Republicans voted to protect their legislative dominance and a concept of limited government which restricts the state and its chief executive from seriously affecting the hegemony of local interests in the formation of public policy.

The Ends of Government: A Difference of Outlook

Behind the conflicting views on fiscal policy and the character of party leadership lie different views on the nature of the political system itself. From James Harrington's *Oceana* to the latest proposal for a constitutional convention in Massachusetts, the basic document of a polity has most often been lifted from the realm of politics to the heavenly city of nonpartisanship where basic agreement on the goals of the state has been assumed *a priori*. Proposals to have the governor and lieutenant governor run as a unit, to abolish or weaken the Executive Council, to lengthen the governor's term to four years, and to permit the governor to reorganize state agencies, subject to legislative veto, are all related to the politics of the major political cultures in the Bay State.

The impetus for constitutional revision through the governor and the party organizations has come from middle-class academicians, professional and businessmen, and civic groups such as the League of Women Voters. Few labor, urban, or ethnic-group spokesmen have been heard in the chorus for change. Indeed, data from a Massachusetts League of Women Voters' questionnaire, presented in Table 8.3, indicate that it is the suburban wings of both legislative parties which are most in favor of revisions. It can be seen in Table 8.4 that in each party's majority group — Yankee Republicans, Irish Democrats — representatives from the traditional and least affluent centers most oppose constitutional revision. Since urban Republicans tend to come from districts with higher socioeconomic status than urban Democrats, the table has sacrificed a number of cases to hold party, ethnicity, and religion constant.

Thirty years ago the Irish Democrats used positions on the Executive Council as a foothold in a Republican and

Yankee-dominated political system. Today, Italo-American representatives occupy a similar minority position. Therefore, it is not surprising to find that only 33 per cent of the responding Italo-American representatives scored "high" on

TABLE 8.3

SUPPORT FOR POLITICAL INTEGRATION AMONG REPRESENTATIVES: BY PARTY AND CONSTITUENCY, 1962

	*High Scores on Constitutional Reform Index**	
Constituency and Party	*Percentage*	*No.*
Suburban Democrats	89	18
Suburban Republicans	73	30
Rural Republicans	65	23
Urban Democrats	33	33
Other representatives†	68	19

Source: Massachusetts League of Women Voters, "Questions to Candidates for General Court," October 1962.

* The items, and the percentages of all responding elected representatives who favored the proposals: abolishing the Executive Council (56%); permitting the governor to reorganize state agencies subject to veto by legislature (75%); and four-year term for governor and other constitutional officers (98%).

† Rural Democrats and Urban Republicans.

TABLE 8.4

SUPPORT OF POLITICAL INTEGRATION AMONG TWO SETS OF REPRESENTATIVES: BY CONSTITUENCY, 1962*

	Yankee-Protestant Republicans		*Irish-Catholic Democrats*	
Constituency	*Percentage*	*No.*	*Percentage*	*No.*
Rural	63	16	50†	4
Suburban	69	24	85	13
Urban	78†	9	21	22

Source: Massachusetts League of Women Voters, "Questions to Candidates for General Court," October 1962.

* Support for all four reform proposals.

† Too few cases for reliability.

the index of constitutional revision or integration compared with 43 per cent of the Irish representatives, 66 per cent of the Yankee lawmakers, and 67 per cent of the Jewish members of the lower house.

The coteries of influentials who operate among the fragmented legislative and administrative chambers most oppose changes that would increase the governor's control over his appointments, departments, and policies. Abolishing the Executive Council, bringing state agencies more fully under gubernatorial supervision, and electing the governor and other constitutional officers for four-year terms, are all likely to diminish the historic pockets of influence. In the contest over the office of Speaker, the supporters of Representative Thompson were least disposed to increase the integrative aspects of state government. In 1964, a proposal to abolish the Executive Council was narrowly defeated by a core-city Democratic and small-town Republican coalition, although

TABLE 8.5

SUPPORT OF POLITICAL INTEGRATION AND VOTE FOR SPEAKER, 1962

(*Figures given as percentages*)

	Support of Political Integration	
Vote for Speaker	*High*	*Low*
Thompson	27	60
Curtis (Republicans)	16	11
Anti-Thompson Democrats	51	18
Not Voting	6	11
	100	100
No. of Representatives	(82)	(57)
Index of Thompson support*	1.09	2.11

Source: Massachusetts League of Women Voters, "Questions to Candidates for General Court," October 1962.

* The index of Thompson support was derived by giving a score of 3 for each Thompson vote, 2 for each Curtis vote, 1 for each no vote, and 0 for each other vote, and then dividing total by number of representatives.

the statutory appointive powers of the Council were curbed by a referendum.

Beneath the data in Table 8.5 lie two views of government. One view, strongly held in the upper-middle-class suburbs, supports an integrative, rational, and managerial political system that gives the governor power to promote statewide public policies. The contrasting view, strongly held in the lower-income, urban centers and small towns, fosters a dispersed, decentralized, and personalized political system in which the General Court and the Executive Council serve as major checks on policy. In this view, reciprocal interests are satisfied and nurture local, communal values — values inherently opposed to the broad policies of the professional bureaucrat and the policy-conscious executive.

CHAPTER NINE

POLITICAL CULTURE IN THE BAY STATE

Massachusetts and the National Political Economy

The roots of this political interpretation lie in the transitions that have impinged on the old characteristics of Massachusetts. Too much emphasis has been placed on the uniqueness of the Massachusetts political culture, its corruption, the alienation of its electorate, and its class and ethnic rivalries. This emphasis has neglected the extent to which forces of the national political economy have eroded regional and state distinctions. At various points in its historical development, Massachusetts has been dominated by the political ethos of the rural, small-town yeomen, the Brahmin patricians, and the urban workers, especially the Boston-Irish community. Today, Massachusetts is part of a post-industrial society that emphasizes technical, clerical, and professional skills to man the burgeoning scientific, defense, educational, and administrative institutions. At the same time, the older industries based on water power, the soil, and unskilled labor are in decline. While the older core cities and small towns have contracted in population and importance, new suburbs of white-collar and professional people have developed.

These transitions have done much to shape the political ideologies of the strata within the state and to give them historical meaning. Thus, the yeoman, patrician, managerial, and worker cultures, each with a distinct political style, are useful constructs with which to assess the new politics of the Bay State.

The Uses of Political History

The investigation of critical Massachusetts elections indicated that the goals and the power positions of the major social strata were significant for an interpretation of such gubernatorial contests. Each election reflected political demands, especially from groups that felt most deprived under the existing political order. Thus, in 1920, the dominant patrician-yeoman coalition imposed its will on the Commonwealth through the Republican Party. Within a decade, urban ethnic minorities had revived a moribund Democratic Party to capture state offices, achieve social mobility, and impose distinct economic and political policies on the Bay State. By 1952, these forces, anchored nationally in the welfare state and locally in the legislature, had lost contact with the growing suburban electorate and its qualitative demands on state government. By 1962, politicians had learned that no governor could gain election unless he made a strong showing in metropolitan areas outside Boston and Springfield. Present-day gubernatorial behavior is very solicitous of new demands for public services, education, and property improvement.

Political Adaptation

Neither party, however, seems to find it easy to adapt to new facts of political life. One reason is the obsessive hold of the older types of political cleavage such as class, region, and ethnicity. To be sure, these remain vital political considerations, especially among Catholic minority groups such as the Italo-Americans who occupy many of the local and state positions in urban centers. But while the evidence indicates the continued existence of ethnic and class bloc voting, discerning politicians realize that in the long run increased demands for quality education and other public services are likely to be the more salient.

A second reason for the gap between political demands and governmental structure is the highly decentralized nature of both political parties. Political power is exceedingly difficult to organize beyond elections, even when, as is seldom the case, agreement exists on how power is to be used.

A third reason for the inability of parties to reflect new demands more readily is that party activity is highly sporadic and consists of small groups functioning as strategic minorities in preprimary conventions, state committee selections, and primary elections. In the past, these strategic minorities and the rules by which they operated placed major power in the hands of the urban Democrats and the rural, small-town Republicans representing the safe areas for each party. One consequence of this rigid structure was that among the inner suburbs of the Boston metropolitan area, the Republicans yielded almost without without a fight to the new Democratic residents. The Massachusetts Republicans are now faced with the same problem that haunts their national party — how to appeal to the metropolitan centers. One time-honored appeal has been to the morality of the Protestant ethos with its safeguard against the moral excesses of economic liberalism; but this appeal tends to wear thin in the eyes of the electorate, and few Republicans can still contend that their party retains any monopoly on middle-class morality.

The art of building durable political coalitions is likely to grow more difficult with time. The old local elites based on social class, ethnicity, and religion are no longer moored to the political order. Moreover, the geographic and social mobility of population reduces the durability of party identifications used in selecting governors and attorney generals. The major development affecting parties is the managerial-progressive demand for institutional reform and greater benefits in metropolitan fringe areas. It is this appeal that is often resisted by politicians in urban centers and small towns.

The Uses of Government

Changes in political culture are manifested in the uses made of political institutions and the movements for their reform. Consider the uses of the governorship in four decades of Massachusetts politics. Before 1928, the governor symbolized a Republican hegemony in which private and public power was effectively blended. A strong or policy-oriented governor was incompatible with the demands of the dominant political strata because an expansion of public power threatened their private domains. Meanwhile, the ethnic groups, who formed the minority Democratic Party concentrated on local offices such as councilman, state representative, and mayor in order to gain a foothold in the system and to provide some degree of social mobility and political leverage.

During the Democratic wave of the early thirties, the governorship became the key instrument for the dispensing of patronage and the formation of economic policy. It was an instrument designed to increase the public power of the labor, urban, and ethnic coalition against the private economic base of the Republican patricians. In both state and nation, the executive formed the pivot for the grand design to circumvent rural-dominated legislatures. Thus James Curley effectively utilized Democratic support in the Executive Council to bypass Republican opposition in the state Senate. In general, gubernatorial hegemony served the interests of the urban Democratic masses while reducing the power exercised by the propertied Republican body and its following of small-town yeomanry — a pattern which lasted through the administration of Governor Paul Dever.

Since the Second World War, the Massachusetts economy

has relied less heavily on a mass industrial base; international issues have altered the technology and skills necessary to run the economy and produce the required administrative, scientific, and consumer services. The manpower and crafts of the core cities and of the countryside are less critical and are, in some cases, irrelevant to the needs of a highly specialized administrative welfare state. At the same time, the Republican yeomen and urban Democrats have gained positions of seniority and influence in the middle echelons of the political system, especially in the legislature. The patricians of the business and financial community no longer supply Leverett Saltonstalls to the Great and General Court. Indeed, both they and the rising managerial strata of the metropolitan fringes are more involved in relating national issues, organizations, and skills to the state level.

The patrician-managerial strata now seek integrated centers of political power within the state to which they can link national policies and economic developments. They find, as has been true for every group seeking reform, that the governorship and the party systems are vital instruments for bringing about rational, managerial changes.

On the other hand, the yeomen and core-city politicians form alliances to protect particularistic economic and social interests with political buffers against the integrated policies being advanced by the upper-middle class. They find, as has been true for every declining social class, that the legislature affords the best opportunity to maintain the values of the status quo. In a word, the politics of the communal interests is to act as a buffer against the fluctuations of a postindustrial economy and a post-rural social order.

The New Massachusetts Polity: Some Future Prospects

If students of American state government were unaware of the immigrants, the urban sprawl, and the problems of the metropolis, they would never dream that foreign affairs and military expenditures could affect the power relationships of the states, their governors, and their citizenry. The American governor has become a buffer between Washington and the states, an intermediary who seeks to secure the highly valued aerospace and electronics contracts, and who also withstands public indignation at higher taxes. In 1962, when half of the governors outside the South were defeated, the major issue was usually taxes. Also, the autonomy of the state and of the chief executive in the state has declined. Moreover, the governors need to find new sources of revenue to meet the drastically accelerating state health, education, and welfare needs, and at the same time need to attract the profitable new industries, and provide public assistance to the casualties of the old, mass-industrial society.

The governor is caught between his suburban, managerial, and yeomen-worker constituencies. The state is a "no man's land" between those groups which most benefit from the affluence of the technical society and those which need protection from its changes.

Whose Responsible Parties?

In recent years, there have been hints that the Massachusetts Democrats might fashion a state party out of the mélange of officeholders, functionaries, and their followings. Only one candidate endorsed in convention was defeated in the 1962 Democratic primaries. The nucleus of a state secretariat has been formed under the guidance of a party chairman with a pipeline to the governor and to a senator in Washington. Fiscal, organizational, and campaign reforms are being initiated. Patronage is being cleared with the party chairman and the local party leaders. However, there was a regression when Governor Peabody was upset in the 1964 Democratic primary by his own lieutenant governor, the growing metropolitan middle class punished the victor, supported proposals for executive reorganization, and, despite a national Democratic landslide, elected Republicans to the three major state offices.

Meanwhile, the once-disciplined Republican Party has lost its cohesiveness. In 1962, two Yankee Republicans challenged the candidates endorsed at the convention, and in all there were three primary fights in the traditionally sedate G.O.P. ranks. Moreover, the advocates of Goldwater, including the Young Republicans, rebelled against the dominance of the Lodge-Herter-Saltonstall patricians. The escalator system for recruiting party and government leaders, campaigning on a unified ticket, and imaginative state committee leadership, all these were in disarray. In the space of one short decade, 1954–1964, Republican strength in the state legislature had declined from 75 per cent to a mere 29 per cent of the seats in the two chambers.

Structurally, the old patrician-yeoman alliance has fallen apart because legislative leaders from the small towns now use their influence to block gubernatorial programs that would shift public costs toward their declining areas and public benefits toward other domains. Rather than join with representatives from Sheffield and Plymouth County in opposition to moderate increases in state taxes, the patricians are caught up in the changing economy as the John Hancock Insurance Company and the First National Bank of Boston cooperate with Harvard and M.I.T. Meanwhile, the old progressive-labor alliance among the Democrats is divided on the issues of more funds for public school education and constitutional revisions to abolish that "Tammany Wigwam" of the less well off, the Executive Council.

Like their regional counterparts in the small-town Midwest, the Massachusetts yeomen may seek to formalize their legislative relations with core-city Democrats. Indeed, a drift in this direction is likely if the central campaign issues are either quality education, mass planning, or the development of the suburban belt. Use of state resources for these objectives involves a relative reduction in funds to maintain core-city interests. Thus, it is precisely on these emerging issues that traditional party coalitions are most subject to revision.

In the old ethnic-labor-urban Democratic coalition the governor was the focal point of economic demands and social recognition. Today, however, the chief executive is often opposed by those with other economic interests: the Great and General Court, the Executive Council, and most state agencies become the union shops for the nonmanagerial strata. They represent the competing, fluid array of old-fashioned capitalists highly exposed to technological risks — the builders, gamblers, small insurance men, and racing owners. They and the other "small businessmen" do not benefit from a managerial economy and a chief executive who promises "good government" and urban renewal in exchange for federal funds and aerospace research contracts.

Socially, the fragmented state government benefits the current minorities. The Italo-American community, for instance, is using the traditional techniques of bloc voting and the patronage of government positions with strong local ties — the Executive Council and the House of Representatives — as a means to protect surplus labor from automation.

America no longer needs bulging muscles and strong backs to lay the rails and dig the canals across an unexplored continent. Crime and corruption are politics by other means, and they are most often engaged in by those in the poorest circumstances. From a middle-class view, government may be fragmented, but from a lower-class view this fragmentation provides the means of official access. For instance, in many urban Negro communities, the professional leaders, like the ministers, are well known by the white community; often great leverage is exerted by less well-known Negro groups such as the ushers' association and the missionary society sisters. The values of ushers and missionary groups are often very different from those of their middle-class clergymen. The power of the legislative parties rests on a social base of such small groups. The groups are often inarticulate, sometimes illegal, and occasionally pawns of the ward boss. In most cases, there is some semblance of grass-roots democracy, although the ushers, the missionaries, and the gambling fraternity have yet to be celebrated in quotations from de Tocqueville or even *The Christian Science Monitor.*

Psychologically, middle-class and working-class values are often defenses against each other. Dominant, cosmopolitan elites and those who have realistic opportunities to join them always fear provincial ignorance that can be turned against them by the demagogue. Those in the most exposed situations usually cut their expectations, develop protective defenses of apathy and cynicism, take refuge in the pseudoequalitarianism of "I'm as good as you are, Buddy, even though you drive a Cadillac." The great fear is proletarianism; this is often a state of mind the possession of which alone may determine membership in the proletariat.

Politically, the managers seek to transform institutions into rational instruments that will cope with public problems. The yeomen and the workers seek to protect the concrete, local situation. The differences cannot be reconciled simply by appeals to middle-class standards because, in that case, gradations of status would be relinquished voluntarily by those who now set the standards. Middle-class Catholics, for instance, tend to have working-class values which impede their mobility. An emphasis on familial values and a de-emphasis on achievement values was universal until this century. Thus, we might end by examining the unusual emphasis placed on work and success since the seventeenth century by some small, northern European, Protestant countries.

In myth, the immigrant was acculturated to American standards, when, in fact, the interaction between host and stranger fashioned a new set of values out of the pliable American ethos. In the same way, no absolute standards of superiority can be placed on the cosmopolitan values of the managers over the parochial values of the yeomen and workers. Nevertheless, the expansion of liberty and a genuine opportunity for meaningful work and self-esteem are most certainly goals of the democratic experiment.

In summary, the major thesis of this book has been that the political cultures of Massachusetts provide a useful and parsimonious key to the development of state government. In essence, the rise of a suburban middle class coincides with the transformation of older agrarian and industrial economies into a national corporate and governmental political economy. The institutions and processes of Massachusetts government have been used as a buffer against these national changes by the strata most adversely affected, namely the yeomen and core-city workers. On the other hand, the style of politics here termed managerial progressivism has been most beneficial to the new middle classes and the Brahmin strata. While traditional ethnic, party, and economic issues are still played out in the political arena, the major issue of Massachusetts can be found in the transformation of its culture and political economy.

This book has also tried to make clear the idea that some observed characteristics of the Massachusetts polity, such as its decentralized party and governmental structures, ethnic politics, and political behavior, have been and still remain useful to older local interests in the state.

In this context, two related structural developments are likely in the continuing development of cultural politics. One is the continuing effort to rationalize the polity in conformity with the premises of managerial progressivism. This can be seen in attempts to secure cohesive political parties, integrate institutions of state government, and increase centralized control in the formulation of education and other public policies. While each issue is determined in a particular context, the trend is toward a continued de-emphasis of the older yeomen and core-city influences on the polity. The major reason for this likely development is that the national political economy is the center of power and decision; a center that no local ethnic, class, or economic group can compete with over time.

Moreover, this projected rationalization incorporating the values of managerial progressivism intensifies a second, related problem. This problem is to provide the political, cultural, and economic attachments for those groups least benefited by the new polity. In the past, the small town's community values, the labor union, the Church, and the urban political machine have sustained these interests. It is clear that their viability has been reduced in the political order and that new public mechanisms must be created to sustain local interests. Therefore, the evolution of new political forms designed to inculcate some semblance of pluralism into state politics stands high on the agenda of public business set by managerial progressives and all thoughtful citizens of the Commonwealth.

SELECTED BIBLIOGRAPHY

Books

Alford, Robert A. *Party and Society*. Chicago: Rand McNally, 1963.

Amory, Cleveland. *The Proper Bostonians*. New York: E. P. Dutton, 1947.

Baltzell, E. Digby. *Philadelphia Gentlemen*. Glencoe: The Free Press, 1958.

Bay, Christian. *The Structure of Freedom*. Stanford: Stanford University Press, 1958.

Bell, Daniel. *The End of Ideology*. Glencoe: The Free Press, 1959.

Burns, James M. *John Kennedy: A Political Profile*. New York: Harcourt, Brace and World, 1959.

Campbell, Angus, Phillip E. Converse, Warren E. Miller, and Donald E. Stokes. *The American Voter*. New York: Wiley, 1960.

Dahl, Robert A. *A Preface to Democratic Theory*. Chicago: The University of Chicago Press, 1956.

Ecclesiastes. 1:10.

Fenton, John H. *The Catholic Vote*. New Orleans: The Hauser Press, 1960.

———. *Politics in the Border States*. New Orleans: The Hauser Press, 1957.

Fuchs, Lawrence H. *The Political Behavior of American Jews*. Glencoe: The Free Press, 1956.

Goodman, Paul. *Growing Up Absurd*. New York: Random House, 1960.

Gordon, Milton M. *Social Class in American Society*. Durham: Duke University Press, 1958.

Hoffer, Eric. *The True Believer*. New York: Harper and Brothers, 1951.

Hofstadter, Richard. *The Age of Reform*. New York: Knopf, 1955.

Hoggart, Richard. *The Uses of Literacy*. New York: Oxford University Press, 1957.

Horowitz, Irving L. (ed.). *Power, Politics and People: The Collected Essays of C. Wright Mills*. New York: Ballantine Books, 1963.

Howe, Irving, and Lewis Coser. *The American Communist Party*. New York: Praeger, 1957.

Huthmacher, J. Joseph. *Massachusetts People and Politics, 1919–1933*. Cambridge: Harvard University Press, 1959.

Jewell, Malcolm E. *The State Legislature*. New York: Random House, 1962.

Key, V. O. Jr. *American State Politics*. New York: Knopf, 1956.

———. *Public Opinion and American Democracy*. New York: Knopf, 1961.

Lane, Robert E. *Political Ideology*. New York: The Free Press of Glencoe, 1962.

———. *Political Life*. Glencoe: The Free Press, 1959.

Latham, Earl and George Goodwin. *Massachusetts Politics*. Medford, Mass.: The Tufts Civic Education Center, 1960.

Lazarsfeld, Paul F., Bernard Berelson, and Helen Gaudet. *The People's Choice*. New York: Columbia University Press, 1944.

Lenski, Gerhard. *The Religious Factor*. Garden City, N.Y.: Doubleday, 1961.

Levin, Murray B. *The Alienated Voter: Politics in Boston*. New York: Holt, Rinehart, 1960.

Levin, Murray B. and George Blackwood. *The Compleat Politician: Political Strategy in Massachusetts*. Indianapolis: Bobbs-Merrill, 1962.

Lipset, Seymour M. *Political Man*. Garden City, N.Y.: Doubleday, 1959.

Lockard, Duane. *New England State Politics*. Princeton: Princeton University Press, 1959.

Merton, Robert K. *Social Theory and Social Structure*. Glencoe: The Free Press, 1957.

Meyerson, Martin and Edward C. Banfield. *Politics, Planning and the Public Interest*. Glencoe: The Free Press, 1955.

Michels, Robert. *Political Parties*. Glencoe: The Free Press, 1949.

Mills, C. Wright. *The Power Elite*. New York: Oxford University Press, 1956.

Rossi, Peter H. and Robert A. Dentler. *The Politics of Urban Renewal*. New York: The Free Press of Glencoe, 1963.

Shills, Edward. *The Torments of Secrecy*. Glencoe: The Free Press, 1956.

Stouffer, Samuel A. *Communism, Conformity, and Civil Liberties*. Garden City, N.Y.: Doubleday, 1955.

Vidich, Arthur J. and Joseph Bensman. *Small Town in Mass Society*. Princeton: Princeton University Press, 1958.

Walker, David B. *Politics and Ethnocentrism: The Case of the Franco-Americans*. Brunswick, Maine: Bowdoin College Government Research Bureau, 1961.

Wilson, James Q. *The Amateur Democrats*. Chicago: The University of Chicago Press, 1962.

Wood, Robert C. *Suburbia*. Boston: Houghton Mifflin, 1959.

Articles and Periodicals

Bazelon, David T. "The Scarcity Makes," *Commentary, 34* (October 1962), 293–304.

Boston Globe. September–November 1962.

Boston Herald. September–November 1928.

The Christian Science Monitor. September–November 1962.

Epstein, Leon. "Size of Place and the Division of the Two-Party Vote in Wisconsin," *Western Political Quarterly, IX* (1956), 138–156.

Fenton, John H. "Ohio's Unpredictable Voters," *Harper's, CCV* (October 1962), 61–65.

Hacker, Andrew. "The Elected and the Anointed," *American Political Science Review, LV* (September 1961), 539–549.

———. "Liberal Democracy and Social Control," *American Political Science Review, LI* (December 1957), 1009–1026.

Hughes, H. Stuart. "On Being a Candidate," *Commentary, 35* (February 1963), 123–131.

Jewell, Malcolm E. "Party Voting in American State Legislatures," *American Political Science Review, XLIX* (September 1955), 773–791.

Key, V. O. Jr. "A Theory of Critical Elections," *The Journal of Politics, 17* (1955), 1–18.

Lane, Robert E. "The Fear of Equality," *American Political Science Review, XLVIII* (March 1959), 35–51.

Litt, Edgar. "Civic Education, Community Norms, and Political Indoctrination," *American Sociological Review, 28* (March 1963), 69–75.

———. "Political Cynicism and Political Futility," *The Journal of Politics, 2* (February 1963), 312–323.

Loughlin, Katherine. "Boston's Political Morals," *The Commonweal, XL* (March 15, 1945), 545–548.

MacRae, Duncan, Jr. "The Relation Between Roll Call Votes and Constituencies in the Massachusetts House of Representatives," *American Political Science Review, XLVI* (December 1952), 1046–1055.

MacRae, Duncan, Jr., and James A. Meldrum. "Critical Elections in Illinois: 1888–1958," *American Political Science Review, LIV* (September 1960), 669–683.

Mallan, John P. and George Blackwood. "The Tax That Beat a Governor: The Ordeal of Massachusetts," in *The Uses of Power,* edited by Alan F. Westin. New York: Harcourt, Brace and World, 1962, pp. 285–322.

Moynihan, Daniel P. "Bosses and Reformers: A Profile of the New York Democrats," *Commentary, 31* (June 1961), 464–465.

New Republic, L (March 1927), 128.

Schickel, Richard. "Soft Advice, Hard Problems" (Review of *The Public Happiness,* by August Heckscher), *Commentary, 34* (October 1962), 357.

Schlesinger, Joseph A. "A Two-Dimensional Scheme for Classifying States According to Degree of Inter-Party Competition," *American Political Science Review, XLVIV* (1955), 1124–1160.

Trow, Martin. "Small Businessmen, Political Tolerance, and Support for McCarthy," *American Journal of Sociology, LXIV* (1958), 275–280.

Reports

The Federal Reserve Bank of Boston. *Annual Report.* 1962.

Boston College-Simmons College Political Survey, October 1962.

Unpublished Material

Hero, Alfred. "Political Attitudes of New England and Other Regions." Paper read at the Conference on Political Extremism in New England, Springfield, Massachusetts, March 1963.

Litt, Edgar. "Characteristics of Non-Voters in Massachusetts." Unpublished MS, 1962.

———. "The Political Perspectives of Jews in an Urban Community." Unpublished Ph.D. dissertation, Yale University, 1960.

Rubenstein, David. "A Study of Voting Patterns in Newton, Massachusetts." Unpublished M.A. dissertation, Boston College, 1962.

Tumavicus, Edward J. "Alienation in the Grocery." Unpublished paper in the Boston College Graduate School, January 1963.

INDEX